Publishers

ZeNaNA Press and Walla

Published by

ZeNaNA Press
20A High Street, Houghton Conquest
Bedfordshire
Telephone/Fax: 01234 740949
Email: steph@cix.co.uk
Website: www.olympicwomen.co.uk

ISBN: 0-9537645-0-8 (England)

Walla Walla Press
P.O. Box 717 Petersham NSW 2049 Australia
Phone and fax: (612) 9560 6902
Email: ascmai@zipworld.com.au
Website: www.asc.zipworld.com.au

ISBN: 1 876718 12 9 (Australia)

Printed and bound in Great Britain by

Priory Press
Boscombe Road
Dunstable, Bedfordshire

First Published 2000

## Copyright

# 'A Proper Spectacle'

# Contents

YALE COLLEGE
LEARNING RESOURCE CENTRE

## Foreword

I was very pleased to be asked to write this foreword. I find it amazing to see how much women's sport has developed and how far we have had to come in order to achieve sporting equality. The book details this struggle through the years and tells the personal stories of some very determined women.

In the sporting arena today women are able to show that they are just as capable as their male counterparts. In Track and Field, women running the steeplechase will finally complete the set. Although naturally not as fast or physically strong as men, women have proved that their qualities of mental strength and their ability to withstand pain are often amazing. They have also demonstrated that female competition can be enthralling to watch.

Going into the Sydney Olympic Games, Marion Jones is attempting to win five Olympic Gold medals - a feat that would surpass anything achieved before - male or female. We have come a long way from the days when married women were not even allowed to watch sporting events.

This book details the struggle for equality in sport. It offers a fascinating insight into the history of both the early and the modern Olympic Games and women's fight for the right to take part in the Games - a fight for which I and countless other women today are extremely grateful!

The bravery, commitment and above all the achievements of these women provide excellent inspiration for the many women competing at all levels in sport today. That we have the right to do this is a very special blessing. We have the chance to go out and prove what we can do - the rest is up to us.

**Paula Radcliffe**
**15th November 1999**
(10,000 metre silver medalist - World Championships 1999)

# Acknowledgements

In addition to all our Olympic women, their families and friends, there are so many other people to whom we are indebted, and without whose guidance, help and support we would never have been able to produce this book.

Anthanassios Tarassoules, Noel Gay, Manfred Seeger, Wolf Lyberg, Greg Moon, Stan Cohen, Ann Hall, Peter and May Heatley, Meg Warren, Gill Livingstone, Angela Rice, Giles Camplin, Den Birchmore, Geoffrey Isles, Ching Lam, Hugh Soar, Hilary Greenland, Roy Simpson (sadly missed), Peter Lovesey, Marco Martini, Roberto L. Quercetani, Eric Cowe, Sandy Duncan, Jos Luypaers, Dave Sheppard - all provided information, inspiration and assistance from afar. Organisations who provided particular help were the Olympic Associations of Argentina, Australia, Great Britain, Germany and the USA. The Croquet Association, the Ballooning Association, Vassar College (USA), Patriomoine Historique (Monte Carlo), the Olympic Museum (particularly Patricia Eckhart and Ruth Beck Perrenoud who made us feel so welcome) and the International Society of Olympic Historians - all provided extensive help.

Tony Bijkerk was always available with a joke or invaluable assistance and Ian Buchanan advised on an early draft, gave us much to contemplate and provided 'impossible-to-find' facts in an instant! Dr Ian Gordon amazed us with his wonderful collection of early swimming photographs, as did Malcolm Fare - the man with a fencing museum in his front room! A team of translators manifested - Stewart Hunt, Tracy Smith, Luisa Cafolla, Ursula Fell, Vivien Buck and Gabrielle Tedder-Douat - all of whom declined to become irritated by our endless 'Could you do just one more letter....?' Exploration of the World Wide Web and other computer mysteries was facilitated by Tracy Mack, Stuart Ward and Pam Woods. In our local area, Shuttleworth Museum, Bedford High School archivist Joan White, Bedford County Archive and our local arts officer, Hilary Western, were all enthusiastic about our efforts when we needed them to be. Eileen Alexander made some timely observations. We would like to mention our dear friends Martin MacDonald (MacDonald Repro) and Debra McGregor (Priory Graphics) who care about what they do and were the only people for the job! Also all the boys at Monographics for their hard work and humour.

Early editing advice was provided by Michael Tedder and Charles Butchart, but the final manifestation must be credited to Jenni Mills who clucked and clucked and sat on the nest when we were itching to leave the coop for a few days. Without Jenni's help in numerous ways we would have been quite lost. In July 1999, Jenni conducted filmed interviews with four of our women Olympians, and we would like to thank David Parker and his Available Light Productions for giving us his camera crew.

We would particularly like to thank Paula Radcliffe who showed much of the "Old Olympic Spirit" so many of our veteran Olympians talked about. These days where money seems to rule so much in all our lives, Paula freely gave her time. She has taken a stand against the use of drugs in sport by wearing a red ribbon whenever she runs. The women featured here would be proud of her, as we are.

Finally, we worked really hard to secure financial assistance for the printing of this book. Just when it looked as though no help was coming, it was befitting that a number of women who believed in the spirit, value and intent of this work came to our aid. Without them, this book could not have appeared in this form. We would really like to thank Lyn Barker, Julie Shipley, Lois Russell, Gabrielle Tedder-Douat and the Bedford Physical Education Old Students' Association for giving us so much and helping us to make this book happen. At the last moment, we received notification that the Millennium Festival Awards For All are supporting the printing of this book. Thank you!

## Photograph Acknowledgements

We have received many personal mementoes and we would like to thank everyone who has entrusted us with their care. Each picture has the following source:

**HM** - Heraklion Archaealogical Museum
**AT** - Anthanassios Tarassoules
**VCR** - Special Collections, Vassar College Libraries, Poughkeepsie, New York
**CA** - Croquet Association
**BHS** - Bedford High School Archive
**MF** - Malcolm Fare
**HS** - Hugh Soar
**IG** - Dr. Ian Gordon
**CM** - Carl Metten
**HW** - Hilke Windh
**USOC** - United States Olympic Committee
**IOC** - International Olympic Committee Museum
**BOA** - British Olympic Association
**ANL** - Associated Newspapers Libraries

**MN** - Maud Nørklit

**BVD** - Bill van Dijk

**NAC** - National Archives of Canada PA151001

**MW** - Meg Warren

**GL** - Gill Livingstone

**TB** - Tony Bijkerk

**MS** - Marie Smit

**SH** - Stewart Hunt

**JB** - Jean Burnett

**SR, JC** - Susan Read and Janet Clerc

**STL** - Sport the Library

**PHM** - Service du Patriomoine Historique Monaco

**HC**- Helen Carroll

**PD** - Pat Down

**DT** - Dorothy Tyler

**CD, JC** - Christine Duggan and Jan Carter

**DC** - Domnitsa Cavanidou

**ES** - Eva Spinks

**BH** - Brenda Halligan

**ME** - Mary Evans

**UF** - Ursula Fell

**AH** - Alice Hodge

**GW** - Gertrude Wilhelmsen

**OZ** - Olympia Zeitung

**TGF** - Tilly Gröte-Fleischer

**ERK** - Elfriede Rahn-Kaun

**AC** - Audrey Court

**MM** - Matilde Moraschi

**VVD** - Vittorina Vivenza Devoti

**SE** - From Sophie Eliott Lynn's book 'Athletics For Women and Girls'

**SD, AT** - Stephanie Daniels and Anita Tedder

**JF** - Despite rigorous attempts to obtain copyright freedom to use this photograph, none was found. It is therefore reproduced with grateful thanks to the photographer, the author and the publisher of Flying and Ballooning from Old Photographs, John Fabb, B.T. Batsford Ltd.

# Introduction to 'A Proper Spectacle'

This book was written on the eve of a new century and of the Sydney Olympics. The year 2000 marks one hundred years of women's recognition as legitimate competitors in the Olympic Games.

There were no women registered as competitors when the first modern Games took place in 1896. Even when their participation was given official sanction in 1900, for many years they encountered incredible opposition to being accepted as serious athletes. Baron Pierre de Coubertin, founder of the Modern Olympics, was himself vehemently opposed to women taking part in competitive sport. In July 1912 he said:

**"Tomorrow, there will probably be women runners, or even women football players? If such sports are played by women, would they constitute <u>a proper spectacle</u> to offer the audience that an Olympiad brings together? We do not think this may be claimed to be so."**[1]

Though we might forgive the Baron his opinion - it was over eighty years ago, after all - he was not alone in his views. At the turn of the century, many doctors believed that if women took part in sport there was a strong chance they would become infertile, and it was a common view that sporting women might even turn into men. It was a time when women could not vote. Their main role in life was to marry and raise a family.

The earliest women Olympians of the modern era were born during this time, so what was it about them that led them to defy convention when so much was against them? We decided to find out by simply asking the women who were there - and so a quest began. We contacted the Olympic Associations of countries whose women took part in the Olympic Games prior to World War II, and asked if they would help us locate their oldest women Olympians. The majority of countries who took part in these games were European. Africa (except South Africa) and most of Asia (with the exception of Japan and Australia) did not feature prominently in women's Olympic competition before World War II.

The Olympic Associations of Greece, Argentina, Australia, Germany, Great Britain, Holland, Sweden and USA helped in the search. We were further assisted by colleagues in the International Society of Olympic Historians and staff at the Olympic Museum in Lausanne who enabled us to track down many of the oldest sportswomen in the world. Initially we sent out a questionnaire and many responded with astounding letters and photographs. This was followed up by telephone conversations and more letters.

Considerable help came from the families of some of the women who were unable to respond personally, either through illness or frailty, but were keen to be included. We were able to visit and record on audio tape the memories of the oldest British women Olympians.

Many of the women who contacted us were extremely generous in what they shared, and some seemed astonished to be asked about their experiences. This was not surprising to us. With a few exceptions, women's Olympic sporting history is not well documented, and published first hand accounts seem very rare. As Physical Education lecturers who had trained during the late 1960s and early 70s, we knew very little about women's sporting history. When we embarked upon this book, we wanted to make a contribution to that history by allowing the women to tell their stories and to set them in their historical context. Incredibly, there are still women with us today who competed in the Olympic Games of 1924! We offer a glimpse of their early lives to try to ascertain who or what influenced them, but primarily we have concentrated on the personal experiences of women competitors in the Games of 1928, 1932 and 1936. Several women comment on shared experiences, yet come at these experiences from different cultures and upbringings. There is richness in both their diversity and commonality.

In a book about sportswomen, there is always the problem of how to name them. Many of those who contributed to this book competed as single women, and have subsequently married. They come from a generation who are accustomed to taking their husbands' names. We have tried to solve the problem simply by calling them the name they competed under and including any other names in the final section and the appendix. This seemed to offer the greatest clarity.

'**A Proper Spectacle**' is not a book concerned with statistics - the National and World records these women held are long since shattered - but it contains historical facts, stories and memories about sports, sportswomen and the Summer Olympic Games that we believe to be important and that have moved or interested us.

In the true Olympic spirit of it being important to participate and not necessarily to win, some of the women featured in this book did not gain medals, and not all made it to the Olympics - but their stories illustrate crucial aspects of women's struggle to participate in sport, and provide a wonderful insight into their lives. The women who played competitive sports in the early part of the twentieth century did so in a climate of unacceptability - Betty Schwartz Robinson's very first women's gold track medal was won when it was still being debated whether or not she should even be there!

This book celebrates these bold spirits who have enabled the women athletes of today to excel.

# CHAPTER ONE - The Earliest Olympics

At the ancient Greek Olympics, any ordinary married woman found *watching* male athletes competing at the Games was in big trouble - she was likely to be taken to the nearby cliffs at Mount Typaneum and thrown off!

Olympic records begin in 776 BC, and tell of a festival of sport and chariot racing which was held every four years at Olympia to honour the god Zeus. Women were not allowed to compete or even in most cases to watch their husbands and sons in action at the games, but indirectly the Olympics owed their existence to a woman. Unless a Priestess of Demeter was present the rules forbade the Games to take place at all. A woman could also attend the Games as a spectator if she were a virgin or, bizarrely, if she were a prostitute. So the average Greek woman had distinctly limited Olympic opportunities. Yet as with so many Olympic tales, even at this time some women achieved remarkable things.

## Boxing - Kallipateria and the first sex test

In 440 BC, a Greek woman called Kallipateria became a boxing coach. Kallipateria was the daughter of an Olympic champion boxer, Diagoras, and her husband, also a boxing champion, coached her son. When he died Kallipateria took over the coaching and her son reached the Olympic final. Even though she knew she risked being thrown off the cliffs, Kallipateria could not resist going to watch her son in the great event so she sneaked in to the Games disguised as a male trainer.

Girls from Ancient Sparta took part in games, throwing, running and wrestling but once married were banished from the gymnasia.

When her son won, Kallipateria could not contain herself and jumped over the wall of the trainers' booth to give her son a celebratory hug. Unfortunately, her disguise fell off and she was recognised. The authorities could not decide whether or not she should be put to death - as a married woman she had committed a crime in witnessing an Olympic event. After some discussion it was decided that she should be saved and pardoned out of reverence for the achievements of her family. To prevent any other unwelcome women sneaking in, a law was passed requiring all trainers to appear naked at the games. This seems to be the first sex test in Olympic history!

## Chariot Racing

If they couldn't compete or watch, women did have one rather more dubious function at the Games - sometimes they were offered as prizes. Originally the Olympic chariot race was a race for suitors and women were won by victorious charioteers. Legend tells that the hero of the siege of Troy, Odysseus, won his bride Penelope in a suitors' race staged by her father.

> **The first person to make a ball to play with was a woman called Angalla of Corcya. Homer recorded the event in the Odyssey.**

But as the games developed, women who wanted to compete found a way around the rules by entering their own horses and chariots. There were no Greek laws to prevent women owning horses and in equestrian events owners, not the charioteers, were proclaimed the victors. This is how Princess Kyniska of Sparta became the very first female Olympic champion, and the first woman to become a champion horse trainer. Though her four horses and chariot won in 392 BC, she was not allowed to be there at the Games or to collect her prize.

> **Princess Nausicaa played the first ball game to be recorded in literature.**
> **Odysseus spotted her playing ball on the shore with her hand maidens during his travels after the Trojan wars.**

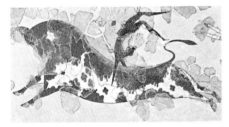

*Bull Leaping (HAM)*

Later, in the first century AD, women also took part in chariot racing. At Delphi there is a statue of the three daughters of Hermesionax who all won events at the Pythian Games, a rival to the Olympics, and one of these girls was a charioteer.

## First Games for Women

> **Women ran for pomegranates!**
> **As symbols of fertility these were prizes in their games.**

The first record of girls participating in their own organised athletic competition was at the games of Hera, which first took place in Greece in 1000 BC and were held every four years, just like the men's games. In a series of races for unmarried girls over various distances, the girls competed wearing a 'chiton', a short tunic which left their right shoulder uncovered to the breast. If they won they received olive wreaths and a share of a cow. The unfortunate cow was sacrificed to the goddess Hera, and the winners were allowed to erect statues of themselves. Unlike the charioteers, it does not seem that they were offered a "beautiful and good man for a husband" in their competitions!

When women's centres for athletics developed on the Greek mainland they were well supported by girls from as far away as Asia Minor who travelled across the Aegean sea year after year to compete in the Festivals.

**Plato considered athletics and horse riding to be suitable activities for women.**

In Greek athletics, most competition for the female sex was for young girls rather than women and it was difficult for girls and women to do anything unless it was first sanctioned by men. There were athletic events and exceptional women, but the Olympic Games went on for twelve hundred years without women competing.

The Olympic Games came to their end as the worship of the old gods became unfashionable. They had become a place for professional athletes and the rewards for success were so great that cheating and bribery were becoming common place. It seemed that the original and true spirit of the Olympics - to excel with honour and friendship - had gone. We would do well today to be mindful of the fate of the early Olympic Games.

## Female Walkers - blazing a trail 1

The Olympic Games disappeared around the end of the fourth century AD and it was not until the late nineteenth century that a movement emerged to reinstate them. But competitive sport would never lose its appeal, and during the intervening centuries women found opportunities to play their part. Country sports at festivals and fairs abounded throughout the world; sometimes women competed for prizes of cheeses, meat or smocks, at other times they were the prizes when male runners ran for a mistress. It was not until the eighteenth and nineteenth centuries that women athletes began clamouring for a share in the sporting limelight with the emergence of trailblazers of all ages who became known as 'female pedestrians'.

The nineteenth century was a time of ideas and 'science'. Doctors, teachers and politicians promoted their beliefs about biological and psychological differences between men and women - differences that sustained male importance, privilege and power. Men were labelled as aggressive, competitive and rational, and women as nurturing, passive and at the mercy of their reproductive systems. Women were encouraged to be genteel in order to preserve their bodies for their main function - to bear children. It was thought that strenuous physical activity was positively dangerous for women. These ideas extended far beyond the sports field, and the theories about women's physical and mental abilities were used constantly and effectively to deny women access to higher education and the vote. A political career was not an option - women were not considered fit for leadership. It was in this climate that the female pedestrians began to stride out.

In England in 1816, Mary Frith, a mother of six, went on a five hundred mile walk at Maidstone. Seven year old Emma Matilda Freeman, from Stroud, regularly completed walks of thirty nine miles around Kent during 1823. Her walks were usually around a quarter mile circuit for wagers of up to £100 and were organised by her father. Matilda's best recorded time was seven hours and forty nine minutes. A sprightly eighty five year old, Mary Kelynack, from Cornwall, also made a name for herself in 1851 when she decided to see the Great Exhibition in London. She thought it could not be much further than Truro, to which she walked regularly, but the actual distance was two hundred and seventy miles and took her five weeks. A week later she walked home! Queen Victoria proclaimed her the most famous woman in England.

The garments women wore were not designed to assist their movement. It was considered shocking for women to show even their ankles. Long distance walking was not confined to England and fortunately, when Amelia Bloomer of New York created her new fashionable 'bloomers,' women were freed from the days of running in smocks and chemise. Mrs. Bloomer visited England in 1851 and was followed by other sportswomen from Australia and America who took up the challenges of long distance race walking.

Their ultimate goal was a challenge made famous by Captain Barclay Allerdice in 1809. The 'Barclay Feat' was to walk a thousand miles in a thousand hours (rest periods were permitted) and a number of women successfully attempted it. The most famous English pedestrian, Ada Anderson, topped the 'Barclay Feat' by walking a mile and a half every hour for 672 hours, covering 1008 miles. As 'Champion Walker of the World' she travelled to New York in 1878 and walked 2,700 quarter miles in 2,700 quarter hours at the Mozart Hall. A craze for six day racing and solo events developed and a record of 409 miles in six days, set by sixteen year old Amy Howard from San Francisco in 1880, was not beaten until a century later in 1984.

Thousands watched and there was much press interest in the women's walks. They were announced daily in the papers and were always for a wager. By the 1880s women's walking dwindled. It was condemned as lewd; race-fixing had crept in and betting was frowned upon. Like the ancient Olympic Games, race walking ceased to be a congenial sport for middle class spectators and competitors once it was no longer respectable.

But women walkers had proved they were sturdy, they had made a contribution to the development of women's athletics and showed a real desire for strenuous competition. Many were working class women who were less inclined to regard themselves as too delicate to sweat. The walkers were the important forerunners of twentieth century women athletes and prepared the ground for the next leap in women's sporting history.

## The Race to Revive the Olympic Games

While women were blazing the walking trail, during the late nineteenth century several men dreamed of reviving the Olympic Games. Evangelis Zappa tried to recreate them at their birthplace, Greece in 1859, but the events were open only to Greeks and were not popular enough to become established.

An Englishman, Dr William Penny-Brookes, believed the sports field could unify youth and all levels of society the world over and had his own vision of an International Olympic Games. He founded the Much Wenlock Festival in Shropshire in 1850, a mixture of athletics and country sports which by 1861 developed into the Shropshire Olympic Games.

**An oak tree planted by Coubertin in 1893 still stands in Much Wenlock.** Unlike the Ancient Greeks, Penny-Brookes thought not allowing women into the stadium lacked gallantry. He himself gave the women the best seats at the Wenlock festivals and encouraged them to take part - even if their only race was for the prize of a pound of tea! A local paper at the time wrote about the women athletes: "They ran well, but how much better they would have done if they had worn bloomers."[1] News of bloomers had reached Much Wenlock, but women there were a little behind the times!

While Penny-Brookes was ready to approach Greece in 1881 to fulfil his international vision for a modern Olympics, a Frenchman, Baron Pierre de Coubertin, was also hoping to revive the ancient Olympic Games. Coubertin hoped that the new Olympics would be an improvement on the ancient ones and, like Brookes, dreamed that the youth of the world would come together in peace, harmony and respect. It was only a matter of time before the two men would meet and share their vision. They became friends and mentors, though they recognised their ambitions were not quite the same.

Coubertin, the younger of the two men, said his games would be "based on conditions suited to the needs of modern life", 2 rather than the country sports of Penny-Brookes. Yet at heart Coubertin was the more traditional, a true Victorian in his attitudes and completely opposed to women's participation in sport. His beliefs were reinforced by the medical profession at the time, who remained convinced of the detrimental effects strenuous exercise would have on women - particularly in child bearing.

Typical of those Victorian physicians was a Dr Robert Barnes, who said in 1873:

> "The functions of ovulation, gestation, labour, lactation, the menopause, in turn all dominate over the entire organism of woman." 3

Therefore it was a woman's *duty* to ensure that she did nothing that might jeopardise her primary function - to reproduce. Sports, it was thought, could interfere with a woman's reproductive system, rendering her useless. A woman's place was at home with a family.

## The First Games of the Modern Olympiad - Athens 1896

In June 1894, the first International Olympic Committee (IOC) was formed at last. It consisted of thirteen European men, predominantly upper-class with the exception of Charles Herbert (Great Britain), a tax inspector, and Jiri Guth-Jarkovsky (Czech), a school teacher. They were to manage all Olympic affairs and were to be responsible for women's participation - or rather the lack of it. Coubertin nominated Demetrius Bikelas, from Greece, as the first president, and Penny-Brookes as an honorary member. But Penny-Brookes' influence was limited, and he died four months before the first Olympic Games in 1896. No women took part in these Games except one, whose participation was unofficial.

## "Melpomene" - A Modern Greek Myth

Christmas 1895 marked a time of great unhappiness for 'Melpomene'. Her seven year old child became gravely ill. Melpomene had to struggle against hunger and poverty every day, but it was too much for a sick child. No Christmas spirit came to help when her seven year old could struggle no more and died.

Melpomene's dark, lively eyes were dulled with grief and she wondered how she would be able to take care of her young baby. She would have to find a way to escape her circumstances if she were to offer her youngest child a better life.

Melpomene lived in Piraeus, the port just outside Athens, and the one good thing about her life was that it had made her tough. When others gave up exhausted from work, Melpomene could keep going. In 1896, news reached Piraeus that a Marathon was going to be run. The Marathon was a famous part of ancient Greek legend which told of an Athenian soldier, Pheippides, who raced twenty six miles to Athens to tell of the Greek victory over the Persians at Marathon. Pheippides fell dead after his effort and all of Greece knew the tale.

'Melpomene' (AT)

Melpomene was walking with her baby in her arms one day when she met a young runner who suggested that running the marathon might be a way for her to become famous and escape her poverty. She already knew that she was a good long distance runner and believed that she had more stamina than many men. The seed of an idea was planted. Melpomene decided to go to Athens and enter the race. She had no money, so she had to walk.

With her toughened feet reddened by the journey, Melpomene reached Athens and told everyone of her plan to enter the race. The story spread until it reached the organising committee of the Marathon, which was part of the newly-revived Olympic Games. They said she was too late to enter - the deadline had passed. But Melpomene was undeterred. She would enter the Olympic Marathon.

On Thursday April 9th 1896, runners began to arrive in the small Greek village of Marathon in preparation for the great race the next day. Melpomene arrived by coach and camped at the place where the race was due to start. She was warmly greeted by the mayor of Marathon, Mr Koutsogiannopoulos. The Greek press was very interested in this peasant woman with her unusual ambition.

Melpomene was lively and quick-witted when she answered the reporters' questions. She told them that she would go after the men even if the committee didn't allow her formally to enter and that she anticipated a time of "Three and two quarters, maybe quicker." To a male runner who said that he was concerned that she would reach the stadium long after the runners had left she said, "Don't insult us women. We have always been top women, while you men have been humiliated by the Americans." [1] She knew all about the recent Olympic defeats the Greek men had suffered at the hands of the USA.

The morning of the race dawned. A service of blessing for the Marathon runners had been arranged, so Melpomene went and asked the priest of Marathon, Papagianni Velioti, to bless her run. He said no - he would only give his blessing at the church of St John to the officially recognised athletes. The service of blessing went ahead without her.

Melpomene came under more pressure from the race committee not to run, but by now they could see how determined she was to take part. They came up with an idea to appease her - they offered to allow her to run in another race with the American team in Athens. Perhaps Papagianni Velioti's refusal to bless her or the pressure exerted on her by the race committee was in the end too much. Melpomene changed her mind. She decided not to follow the Marathon race on Friday 10th April.

The men set off at 2.00 p.m. and on that afternoon a new Greek hero was born. Farmer Spyros Louis knew the race's rough terrain and timed his effort perfectly to win the race. Wild celebrations broke out in Athens, and even the King ripped off his hat and waved it madly at the crowds.

On the first morning that Spyros Louis awoke as a modern Greek legend, Melpomene ran the Marathon distance on her own. She set off on Saturday 11 April at 8.00 am. Knowing that if she were successful her feat would not be believed, she asked a teacher, a magistrate and a mayor to witness the time she started and to sign a piece of paper to that effect - and Melpomene did it. She ran the Marathon distance.

She reached her destination in Athens at 1.30 p.m. (having stopped to look at some ships on the way) and asked some non-commissioned army officers to sign the paper she had carried with her. They asked her why she had run such a distance, to which she replied, "So that the King might give my child a position in the future." [2]

In fact the myth happens to be a true story. It was against great opposition that this brave woman called 'Melpomene' ran the Marathon unaided, alone and successfully. Like many other women in history, her extraordinary achievement was never recognised.

Melpomene's real name was Stamati Revithi and it is only recently that her real name has been re-claimed. After her marathon run, athletics officials couldn't remember her name so they labelled her 'Melpomene', who is the Greek muse of Tragedy. Looking at Stamata Revithi, all they could see was a tragedy, not an extraordinary feat. Though Stamata's life was tough and the loss of her child undeniably tragic, she was also a determined, athletic woman whose achievement was both forgotten and discounted. Stamata's run symbolises not just a fighting spirit, but the determination of a mother to care for her children and escape her circumstances. In many ways she had no alternative but to run.

The Greek man Spyros Louis who won the marathon of 1896 was famous for the rest of his life. He was even invited to the Berlin Olympic Games of 1936 and presented an olive branch from his home village as a symbol of peace to the man who opened the games, Adolf Hitler. The Greek woman who also ran a marathon, Stamata Revithi - 'Melpomene'- was never heard of again.

# CHAPTER 2 - Paris 1900:
## The First Official Olympics Games For Women

After years of planning and effort, Pierre de Coubertin's dream of reviving the Olympic Games had come to fruition. Coubertin had become President of the International Olympic Committee just as the first games of the modern Olympiad took place in Athens in 1896, and he was already planning for the second modern Olympic Games to be held in Paris in 1900. It was to be a long time, eighty-seven years, before any women would become a member of that Committee.*

1900 was also the year the World Exhibition was scheduled to take place in Paris, with celebrations and events akin to our own Millennium celebrations. The Olympic Games were taking place at the same time, from 14th May to 28th October, and were considered by many to be part of the World Exhibition. Consequently some of the competitors did not know if they were in the Olympic Games or the World Fair.

Happily for the women athletes of the time, the International Olympic Committee had little influence in Paris. The organisers of the World Exhibition seemed unconcerned about the rights and wrongs of women competing in sport.

To this day there is still confusion as to which events were Olympic and which were World Fair events, so it remains a matter of personal opinion and debate as to who the first female Olympic competitor and champion actually was.

For a sport to be Olympic in 1900 it had to be an open sport, amateur and international, not handicapped and not motorised. The long-held view was that women took part in just two Olympic sports in 1900 - tennis and golf. Latterly, sports historians have accepted that women were involved in the yachting. Old programmes of the Paris Exposition show that women participated in ballooning, croquet, equestrianism, golf, tennis and yachting. Bearing this in mind, we take the view that all women who took part in these sports (which were open, amateur, international, and neither handicapped nor motorised) were Olympians.

*FOOTNOTE: Pirjo Haggman and Flor Isova Fonesca became the very first female members of the IOC in 1981. In the allegations of corruption that rocked the IOC during 1998/9, Flor and Pirjo did not escape scrutiny. Pirjo resigned rather than face an enquiry into her alleged acceptance of bribes over the Salt Lake City bid. Flor was not implicated and is still a member of the IOC.

# Croquet

The women who competed in Paris in 1900 took part in sports that were socially acceptable - sports which were not considered to be too strenuous. Competitors were seen as elegant and certainly not aggressively competitive. The first Olympic women competitors were genteel ladies who had time and money to follow leisure pursuits.

**An ingenious wire cage, an anti-Aeolian, was developed to keep a lady's voluminous crinoline skirt in trim during play.**

No one knows for certain when croquet was first played, but it was spotted by a Miss Macnaghten in the North of France in 1830, where country folk played with bent willow boughs for hoops. It was very soon seen on the lawns of England when she brought the game home. The very first croquet clubs had been formed in the 1860s, and the game rapidly grew in popularity amongst the moneyed classes. It was very much a 'lady's' game - a ball game

**Croquet features as a popular sport in 'Little Women' by Louisa M. Alcott.**

which ladies were allowed to play because it did not raise either perspiration or hemline! As women often played with one hand on the parasol it was seriously debated in the early days as to whether men should play one handed too.

The Indian rubber mallet had a great role in the development of the women's game. It did not require the muscles of a strong man to wield and croquet proved to be a game from which women were not incapacitated physically. For women to be able to take part in a game in the open air, and alongside men, was a novel experience, and croquet became both fashionable and social.

The view that women were passive and not really interested in competition was very strong at this time. But as anyone who has ever played it knows, it is only on the surface that croquet seems genteel and 'lady-like'. If a mild form of croquet never threatened traditions or masculinity, tournament croquet transformed the game. 'Crinoline croquet'

**In the USA the Boston clergy were opposed to croquet on the grounds that it promoted licentiousness on the lawns.**

developed into a serious sport at which the women were often as good as the men. It was as popular to watch as to play, with tournaments in particular drawing large crowds of spectators. The first Lady Championship of England was held in 1869.

*Miss Maud Drummond, Lady Croquet Champion of England, 1897 (CA)*

For women, croquet was an acceptable start to their competing with and against men in sport - but it was not always a success in their relationships! The International Herald Tribune of 29th October 1909 reported on a case for a judicial separation, brought by Mrs. Alice Mary Fearnley-Whittingstall against her husband, a man of the cloth who seems to have been singularly lacking in the Christian virtues of tolerance and humility whenever croquet was the issue :

> *"It was alleged that the rector frequently lost his temper, and his wife had stated that on one occasion when they were playing croquet he was so annoyed because she raised a question as to whether his ball had quite gone through a hoop that he did not speak to her for days."*[1]

The judge, Mr. Justice Bargrave Deane, remarked, "I do not think there is any game which is so liable to put one out of humour as croquet." It began to get less popular as more exciting sports came in and it had its critics - if only from the archery enthusiasts!

> *"Croquet is objectionable for two reasons. The first is that, since ladies will wear corsets, stooping is to them a very unwholesome act, causing a pressure upon organs of the body very sensitive and easily injured. The second is that the effort of muscle required is too slight for working any appreciable benefit even to active members."* [2]

Very little is written about the first and only Olympic croquet competition of 1900. An expensive sand court was built specially for the occasion in the Cercle du Bois de Boulogne. Play started on Wednesday 24th June and continued every Sunday thereafter until 15th August, which is probably why there were no international players and few spectators. It is thought there was just one paying spectator, an Englishman and lover of the game, who watched the early matches of the competition. In all there were four croquet events and twelve competitors, all French, and just three women playing: Madame Brohy, Mademoiselle Ohnier and Madame Depres. The women competed on the 28th June in two events against men, singles with one ball and singles with two balls. Neither Madame Brohy nor Mademoiselle Ohnier progressed to the second round and Madame Depres did not finish the event. Not, perhaps, a remarkable start for women, but to play competitively and *on equal terms with men* in the Olympic Games is a feat rare in any sport in any century, even today.*

*FOOTNOTE: One of the few Olympic events in which women have competed on equal terms alongside men is shooting, but after Zhang Shan, a female Chinese skeet shooter, had beaten men to win Gold in 1992, the International Shooting Union ruled against mixed competition.

## Tennis

There is certainly no dispute that tennis ranked as an Olympic sport in the Paris Games of 1900. Although there was only a small women's entry of six,
the standard was high with all the top international players competing, including British Wimbledon Champion Charlotte Cooper, the USA Champion,

> Tennis was first called sphairistike! The name 'tennis' seemed a better name - it was easier to remember and spell.

Marion Jones, Helene Prevost of France and Hedwiga Rosenbaumova of Bohemia, both leading players in Europe.

> **Tennis**
> "For a game imposing so much a strain on the human brain as well as on the body, a woman is simply too weak. As to the brains required in the process, hardly any woman would be capable of even mastering the game's counting system."

Tennis has a long history as a sport. Romans, monks and medieval players all had their own form of tennis and it was called a "naughty and unlawful game" by Sir Thomas Moore in his 'Utopia'. Modern tennis as we now know it was 'invented', or rather adapted and patented, in 1873 by an Englishman, Major Wingfield. It was a woman, Miss Mary Outerbridge, who introduced it to America in 1875 after she had seen the British Army playing tennis in Bermuda. Until then, croquet had been the front runner in mixed sporting competition (and also in courtship!) but its vast numbers of followers were beginning to see it as too simple, and were looking for a more challenging game.

Women had taken part in tennis from the very beginning, so there were few debates and obstacles to their playing, apart from dress codes - always provided they played in the seclusion of their own country houses and did not neglect the kitchen and the nursery. When they emerged from the house demanding to be admitted to the lawn tennis club and play in tournaments, they were not quite so favourably accepted.

Dublin staged the first tennis tournament open to women in 1879. The winner was Miss M. Langrishe, who also won in 1883 and 1886. The top English (croquet) club, Wimbledon, rejected women tennis players at first but relented in 1884 when they introduced their own ladies' tournament - yet it was still unseemly for women to play anything too strenuously or competitively.

*One of the earliest tennis matches at Vassar 1885 (VCR)*

Though women's competitive tennis had begun, it was advocated that they play their matches at different venues away from the crowds and after the men had finished. A resolution approved by Bedford Riverside Tennis Club on 17th March 1913 did give women one advantage - they allowed lady members to be provided with three 'best balls' free of charge, whilst the men had to pay 9d for each ball!

In the Paris Olympic Games of 1900, women's tennis was played at the same venue as the men's, at the Ile du Puteaux Club in the middle of the river Seine, ironically Pierre de Coubertin's own tennis club. The event took place between July 6th and 11th with six women competing in the singles. Charlotte Cooper beat Helene Prevost in the final to win the first Women's Olympic tennis title, and the very first Olympic gold in a women-only event.  She also won the mixed doubles title with Reginald Dougherty of Great Britain, making her a double gold medal winner.

Like croquet, women's tennis was not included in the St. Louis Olympics of 1904 and it had a chequered Olympic future.  It was re-introduced in 1908 in London.  France and Great Britain shared the women's titles until 1924, when the great Helen Wills won for the USA  Women's doubles were introduced in the 1920 Games. After 1924, *all* Olympic tennis came to a halt when the International Tennis Federation passed a rule forbidding its members to play in the Olympic Games. Not happy to allow the IOC to organise a tennis tournament which might rival its own, and with unresolved questions about professionalism, this decision caused one of the few socially acceptable women's games to be withdrawn from the Olympics until 1988.

*Overhead smash 1891 (VCR)*

# Ballooning

Over thirty balloons took part in free ballooning events during the Olympic Games and Paris Exposition between the 17th June and 12th October 1900.

People have always dreamed of flying, but it wasn't until the eighteenth century that constructions were designed that could take to the air. France has a history of achievement in ballooning. The famous balloonist Montgolfier brothers, Stephen and Joseph, first devised balloons made of paper, then progressed to balloons which carried animals, and finally people. Amazingly, neither of the Montgolfier brothers left the ground, preferring to leave the testing of their designs to those more adventurous (or foolhardy).

Ballooning was a sport in which women participated almost from the beginning. Early women balloonists went skyward wearing all their finery and so the dictates of current fashion were not a disability. In 1784, French women at the court of Louis XVI, the Contesse de Montalembert and Mademoiselle de Lagarde, took to the air on one of the early Montgolfier voyages.

There were several women pilots during the nineteenth century, one of whom, Jeanne Garnearant, parachuted from her basket over Paris. Jeanne **The first aerial photo was taken from a balloon in 1858 above Paris.** ballooned for a thirty six year period and flew all over Europe. At the turn of the century there was an upsurge of interest in high altitude research, and recreational ballooning as a sport became very popular. The landed gentry had their own balloons, often employing pilots to fly them, and women frequently accompanied their fathers or husbands.

In the distance and endurance discipline for top balloonists in Paris on 9th-11th October 1900, the first and, as it turned out, the only Olympic female balloonist took part. French balloonist Madame Maison sailed for 11.38 hours and covered 650 kilometres from Paris to reach Keulroth, in Silesia, as an assistant to her husband. They came in fourth.

Ballooning was never contested again in any Olympic Games.

## Women Balloonists

"And now let us grumble a little, if we may. First against women. They go up in balloons a lot. They even do their utmost to break open their heads in air-planes....their participation in celestial races must be prohibited by police laws in the absence of club rules. Let women accompany their husbands every now and then, that is quite enough. It is said the other day in Paris, the aeronautic society that has the lovely name of Stella and has only female members saw twelve or thirteen balloons taking off piloted by women. This sight would not have been to our liking.... in order to make a good pilot one needs calm, "sang-froid", self-control, calculated will-power made of prudence and energy.... a whole array of qualities which are very much appreciated in a man, but very unpleasant in a woman. And also, really, if a woman is still young enough to like going up in a balloon and to follow her penchant....it is because she does not have much to do at home...."[1]

Pierre de Coubertin, August 1911

## Yachting

Sailing has had a significant influence on the development of civilisation and by custom sailing vessels have been called 'she'. In 4000 BC the Egyptians used sails on boats for commerce, fishing and warfare, and later sailing for pleasure developed. Initially yachting was restricted to the court and the wealthy, but once sailing became a recreational activity it was only a matter of time before it became a sport for women too. Women 'mastered' the science of navigation, and were no longer prepared to be mere passengers while the skipper had all the fun. Indeed many women became addicted, finding in their yachting achievements both acceptability and respect. Keen sailor and five times Wimbledon champion, Lottie Dod, chose to sail with friends off the Western Coast of Scotland in 1889 rather than defend her tennis title that year because she said she was having such a good time.

There were no women's yachting events in Paris 1900, but like croquet and ballooning, yachting was an 'open' sport, with men and women competing together. On May 22nd on the river Seine, the Countess de Pourtales was able to sail on the 'Lerina' for Switzerland with her husband to win her first race, followed by another victory on 23rd June and a second place on 25th June - two Olympic gold medals and a silver. Helen de Pourtales is the very first woman

Olympic medalist in a mixed event, and, by participating on May 22nd, the very first woman Olympian.

In the 1904 Games there were no yachting events at all, but in 1908 another woman, Frances Rivett-Carnac from Great Britain, crewed with her husband in the seven metre class aboard the 'Heroine' and won the Olympic gold medal. Dorothy Wright (Great Britain) was the only woman to compete in the yachting event in Antwerp, 1920, and won a gold medal as a crew member aboard the 'Ancora', owned jointly by her father and husband.

In 1948 the IOC belatedly voted to allow women in future yacht racing as part of a mixed or female crew - they were allowed in 'officially' in 1952, 52 years after their first gold medal!

## Golf

The exact date of the founding of the ancient game of golf is a disputed point but there is no doubt that in early times golf resembled a wilder form of croquet.

> **Mary Queen of Scots played golf the day after her husband had been murdered - when she should have been mourning.**

A forerunner of the game was popular among the Romans, and in Holland and Belgium during the 14th Century the mode of play and the 'weapon' used were not unlike that of today. Scotland became the home of golf, where it was much played during the 16th Century.

> **In 1810 the earliest recorded golf competition was held for local fishwives in Musselburgh near Edinburgh.**

During the industrial age golf's popularity grew, though in the late 1880s and 90s there were very few golf clubs that would admit women as members (today there are still some clubs where women are not welcome) and there was no major women's golf tournament. Despite this, there was a growing interest amongst many women in pursuing the sport.

> **Catherine of Aragon is the first recorded female golfer. She wrote in her diary that she found time to play golf during a period of political inactivity in 1523 - it probably took her mind off divorce and husband Henry.**

Most clubs were willing to allow women to accompany men to the course, but they were not expected to venture onto the hallowed turf or to play serious golf. When women's courses were first started they were conspicuous for their shortness and lack of hazards, and it was thought a wooden putter would be sufficient over any obstacle encountered during the round. But women's ambitions were not satisfied, and they demanded longer holes and more challenges, with real sand in the bunkers. Despite the doubts of men that women would ever become proficient, the women golfers soon proved they were strong and could play properly. Some men's clubs encouraged women, but separate women's clubs were also established to overcome male prejudice and to promote the women's game. Eventually the Ladies Golf Union was formed in England in 1893, and a National championship introduced.

**'Miss Higgins' is no lady but an elastic attachment invented by a top American player to stop ladies' voluminous skirts flapping in the wind.**

This was the beginning of women's golf as a serious sport, and it was included in the Olympic Games of 1900.

*Vassar College students playing golf 1898 (VCR)*

Ten women contested the Olympic Golf competition on October 3rd in Paris, four American and six French women. The Americans took the first three places and the winner was Margaret Abbott, a champion golfer back in America who was studying Art in Paris at the time and entered after reading about a golf competition. Margaret, who played in sensible, comfortable clothing which allowed for movement and swinging a club, claimed her success was due to the fact that the French competitors wore high heels and tight dresses - highly impractical Olympic clothing which undoubtedly gave Ms Abbott the edge!

It is thought that up to the day she died she never knew that she was the first American Olympic female winner. Women golfers never played in the Olympics again.

## Equestrianism

Sporting events featuring people in partnership with horses had a long history in the Ancient Olympics, although horse riding was never as popular as chariot racing. Equestrianism is one sport where there has never been any dispute about women's ability. Boadicea (or Bouddicca), who died in AD 62, was the first British Queen to maintain a riding stud, and she is said to have driven in chariot races and to have bred horses for export to Rome. Lady Godiva rode naked on her white horse through the streets of Coventry, England, in the 11th Century as a protest against the tax on horses. In France Joan of Arc led her troops to battle on horseback, and American pioneer women travelled thousands of miles on horseback or driving covered wagons with their families to settle in unknown country.

In the 16th century, equestrian competition developed in riding schools in Vienna and Naples as military training. Racing across ditches, fences and hedges became the steeplechase we know today, and a popular sport in Ireland and England. Showjumping, originally over a single fence, had its first International event in Paris in 1866, while dressage, a training method for horses, remained exclusively military and for commissioned male officers only. As hunting and racing became pastimes for the wealthy, women developed both passion and skill for the sports and rode and competed alongside men.

**Racing is called the sport of Kings, but Queen Anne founded Ascot and Queen Victoria kept up the Royal Stud at Hampton Court.**

Equestrianism appears on the programme as an official Olympic event in Paris, 1900, but women are not credited with having taken part.

On a visit to the Olympic Museum in Lausanne in February 1999, we discovered a reference [1] to Mademoiselle Elvira Guerra and it would seem that she joins the marathon runner Stamata Revithi as another forgotten Olympian.

Elvira Guerra competed for France on her own horse, Libertin, in the Chevaux de Salle (Hacks and Hunter Combined) event on 31st May, though she was not placed. Elvira is the second woman to compete as an individual in a mixed Olympic event and may have been overlooked in the search for the first women Olympians. She competed just nine days after yachtswoman Helen de Pourtales (mixed event gold medallist), and several weeks before tennis player Charlotte Cooper (the first gold medallist in a woman's event), golfer gold medallist Margaret Abbott, intrepid balloonist Madame Maison, and the croquet players Madame Brohy, Mademoiselle Ohnier and Madame Depres.

After Elvira competed in 1900 it proved surprisingly difficult for women to make the breakthrough into Olympic competition, perhaps because equestrianism as a sport had its roots in military training long before women were accepted into the armed forces.

Outstanding British rider and just fifteen years old, Helen Preece applied to compete in the Modern Pentathlon at the Stockholm Games of 1912. In New York at the Madison Square Horse Show, Helen Preece had already won the $1000 Gold Cup and was experienced in shooting, cross - country, fencing and swimming. With boundless enthusiasm she trained for 6 hours a day, in preparation for the Olympics. About the modern pentathlon events and the forthcoming Olympic Games, she said:

> *"A formidable list, you will agree, and all have to be won, but my*
> *father and friends, under whose guidance I am now undergoing*

*quite an arduous course of training, seem to have every confidence in me, and of course, I myself am enthusiastic. I have obtained special leave of absence from my school in Hertfordshire, and my day's work now commences as early as 5 o'clock every morning and only ends with bedtime at 8 o'clock. A varied programme is mapped out for me each day, but it always includes riding, shooting, swimming, running and walking practice, and today I have been put on a special diet, also, so that I should be absolutely fit for the Pentathlon on July 11th. The one thing that worries me is the fact that I shall be the only woman competitor in this particular contest; it may make me nervous"* 2

Writing in the 'Olympic Review' of July 1912, President Coubertin wrote that a registration had been received, signed by a 'neo-Amazonian' who aspired to compete in the Modern Pentathlon - he was referring to Helen Preece. The Swedish Olympic Committee was free to reject or accept Helen's registration. There were no rules or legislation stipulating women could not compete, but Coubertin's opinion won the day. The Swedish Olympic Commitee refused Helen Preece's application, saying it would be impossible to accept a woman competitor in the sport.

As late as 1948 the International Equestrian Federation refused entry to women in the London Games, but slowly moved with the times and admitted women to the Olympic dressage in Helsinki 1952, and into showjumping in Stockholm in 1956, four years later. Great Britain's Sheila Willcox, Badminton Champion of 1956, '57 and '58, was nonetheless refused entry to the Olympic Three Day Eventing competition in Stockholm.

All equestrian events are now open - men and women compete together on equal terms. At the centenary of women's participation in Sydney 2000, the very first Modern Pentathlon for women will be held, which includes equestrianism. Perhaps we should think of it as a tribute to one of the first and forgotten women Olympians of modern times, Elvira Guerra and the 'neo-Amazonian' fifteen year old, Helen Preece.

# CHAPTER THREE - Preparing For Glory

The women who competed, officiated or spectated in 1900 were not thrown off any mountains for their audacity, but women still had many mountains to climb before they were accepted as athletes and achieved the highest accolade for any sportsperson - to be an Olympian.* Through luck and daring, women had arrived at the Olympics, but the founder of the modern Games, Pierre de Coubertin, came out increasingly against their participation.

Coubertin claimed that women's sports might even be against the laws of nature, and that women sledding was "the most unaesthetic sight human eyes could contemplate." *1* He once said that female applause should be the reward for male athletes - he could not see that women might want to compete themselves nor that exercise might be good for them.

## Votes and Games For Women

Coubertin was not alone in his views. Many men and even women shared his perspective, but groups of women within society were striving for change. Most notable amongst these were the suffragettes who fought for the right

for women to vote. They tied themselves to railings and were imprisoned, assaulted and force-fed. They believed that protest and resistance were the only means they had to sway public opinion and to change the law quickly to win the vote.

Sports were important to the suffragettes. In 1908 in London, Emmeline Pankhurst and her suffragettes threatened to disrupt the London Olympic Games if the organisers ceded to the IOC and refused

*With megaphone and leaflets suffragette Miss Manners ascended in a balloon for the opening of Parliament in 1909 (JF)*

women's entry. Another tactic they used was to dig up golf courses and leave the message, 'No Votes, No Golf.'

* FOOTNOTE Modern professionals like tennis player Steffi Graf have competed in the Olympics solely to win this honour.

The outbreak of World War I in 1914 meant that women worked away from home to contribute to the war effort. They sweated in factories, drove ambulances and took on 'men's' work simply because the men were all fighting. They supported their families and became aware of their own abilities - this sowed the seed for social change, and women's attitudes to themselves were altered.

They had experienced economic independence, though after the War many women who worked in industry gave up their jobs to the returning men.

Women had shown that they were capable of doing all kinds of work and assuming all kinds of roles - yet it took a long time to alter the view that women were primarily wives and mothers who were in danger if they took part in strenuous sports.

British athlete, Vera Searle Palmer (1901-1998) competed during the 1920's. On a recording she made in 1990, Vera said:

> "I would think it would be safe to say that 99% of the medical profession in this country were against women taking an active part in athletics. They said you were leaving your womanhood on the track, and it was quite possible none of us would ever have children. That made me laugh. How could they know anything about it? They'd never seen any women running, either before or after their races. Married women were frowned on. When I defended my club championship as a married woman I lied to my husband and I took my kit with me to compete. When my husband found out he didn't speak to me for 3 weeks. I think it was because I lied to him and not because of competing. When my first child was born in 1928 they thought I would have a difficult time."

## Early Training

Immediately before and after the First World War, arguments still raged about which Olympic sports women should be allowed to compete in. Whilst the debate went on, a new generation of women like Vera Searle-Palmer were quietly getting on with preparing themselves for international sporting competition. It is amongst this generation that we find the oldest surviving women Olympians today, many of whom were prepared to share their memories with us.

But what was it that prompted these women to dare to aspire to Olympic glory, at a time when so few voices were raised in their favour? The obstacles they had to overcome simply to train for competition were enough to daunt the doughtiest spirit. What is interesting is that many of the women had families and male figures (most coaches were men) who were very positive about their sporting aspirations. Several had sporting fathers who trained them - somehow, these men did not share the views of Baron de Coubertin or those others who wanted to keep women off the sports field.

### Violet Webb, Great Britain, Hurdler, 1932 and 1936 Olympics.

"My father spotted my talent and he made a complete flight of eight hurdles which we kept at the ladies' changing rooms at Paddington recreation ground. I jumped high over them as it hurt when you hit the solid barriers! I broke my arm once doing the hurdles, those awful hurdles. It didn't deter me, I went straight back again. The hurdles were formidable, people have no idea, I have to show people pictures of them because they don't believe me!

*Violet Webb - World Record, Hanover 1931 (SRJC)*

There was a master who ran the Willesden athletic club after school. Then a lady wanted me to join the Ladies Polytechnic, in Regent Street. Being tall, they said have a go and they just put me in the hurdles. I joined the club. There were lots of well known clubs, ours was one of the poorer clubs athletically but I stayed with it. They helped me in the early days. I trained twice a week and Sunday mornings. My father trained me.

In my first International in Germany at 16, I won and I equalled the existing world record of 12 seconds. I just loved the sport. When you're young you just take it in your stride, but people thought it was terrible for women to compete. But I thought that was stupid. I didn't take any notice what they thought. It was my life then."

*Fernanda Bullano, Italy, Sprinter 1936 Olympics.*

"My father was an athlete and when I was in the Venesi Unica Club a female athletics group was just being set up. My father suggested I enrol and so - without realising - I became an athlete. In 1930, no-one talked about women in sport. We rarely bought a newspaper, it cost twenty cents, and we were so poor, we didn't even have a radio."

*Audrey Brown, Great Britain, Sprinter 1936 Olympics.*

"My parents never saw any difference between my taking up athletics and my brothers doing so, but my other middle class relatives and family friends were not so accepting. I had four brothers* who were all keen sportsmen and above average athletes and I played in various school teams but no athletics were included at school. I took it up at University and was immediately successful. I was fortunate that at University there was no difference in the attitude towards men and women in athletics. In addition I was fortunate to live near a club like Birchfield Harriers.

*Audrey Brown training with older brother Ralph (left), international 400 metres hurdler, and younger brother, Godfrey (AC)*

Except for London, there were few clubs for women and as a result there were not many inter-club competitions."

*Eva Dawes, Canada, High Jumper 1932 Olympics.*

"My father was quite an athlete for a time. I think it was him that pushed me into it. Where we lived we had a ravine at the back of the house and my father dug up a space and got some stands and cross bar and started training me out there. To make me get over the bar he used to put 25 cents on the bar and said, 'You get over that, you can have this.'"

* FOOTNOTE Audrey's brother A.G.K. Brown, won a gold medal in the 4 x 400m and a silver in the individual 400m in Berlin in 1936.

### Maud Sundberg, Sweden, Sprinter 1928 Olympics.

"In Sweden we have school competitions every Autumn with competitors from all over Sweden. My school headmaster had found that I ran faster than the others so he asked me to start in the 60 metres, which I won with a new school record. So it started, and I saw the possibility of going abroad in the future.

A girl friend and I walked a mile* two or three times a week to swim in a lake, and on our way back we ran between every telegraph post. I started like the runners from Kenya! We had a lot of difficulties. By introducing athletics for women in Sweden, people thought it would give us muscles like men. Women should be "Standing in the kitchen and bearing children!" was a common saying. From the 1926 Women's World Games in Gothenburg and in other connections with English sportswomen I found that their opinion on this matter was different. I hope that nowadays we are on the same level."

As Maud was discovering, it was in athletics that women faced the toughest fight of all to win acceptance. But it was no less difficult for others. Although swimming was one area where women were beginning to be accepted as competitors, as we shall hear later, mixed bathing was still looked on with suspicion right up until the First World War and beyond. So it was something of a challenge for female 'water-babies' to find sufficient time at a pool when they might train.

*Jean McDowell, Scottish champion and record holder (JB)*

### Jean McDowell, Great Britain, Freestyle Swimmer 1928 Olympics.

"I was spotted swimming at North Berwick when I was down on holiday by McCracken (a professional swimming coach) and he said to my Father, 'If you give me that girl to train I'll make her a world champion.' I thought my coach McCracken was gospel but looking back I don't think he had much of an idea or knew very much more than me. In those days, there was no mixed bathing, so the ladies of the Warrender Club (Edinburgh) had Saturday mornings, and of course all the school kids were there. You'd just do what you could - there was no idea that I, as an Olympic hopeful, must have room to swim! We just swam up and down - there was no training like you people do today. We had a stopwatch but times never meant very much in a sixteen yard pool."

* FOOTNOTE A Swedish mile is around 6 English miles

*Joyce Cooper, Great Britain, Freestyle and Backstroke Swimmer 1928 and 1932 Olympics.*

"My training started in the sea. We left Ceylon after the 1914-18 war, and in 1925 I was staying in Eastbourne and I went down to my local pool where I saw Vera Tanner swimming - she'd been in our Olympic team in 1924. She was doing the crawl which was quite new then, and I thought 'Oh! perhaps I'll do that.'

My one ambition was to beat her. Through watching her everything snowballed for me and I found myself in the European Championships. One day poor Daddy, who helped me, wanted to time me. We had to traipse all over London to try to find a pool that had mixed bathing. When we found one they said he would have to get into a bathing costume and they togged him out in one of their all-in-one costumes with blue and white stripes and the name of the bath on it. He was six foot two and thin - they called him Spindles! I can see my Daddy standing there to this day!

*Joyce Cooper (IG)*

My coach, old Howcroft, was the best in the world at that time. All during my swimming career he was wonderful and a darned good trainer. I was supple but not strong, I had no strength in my legs and back, and my arms were weak. I was knock-kneed and loose limbed - my legs went in all directions. I couldn't climb a rope and fell off a bar if I got on it! He gave me strength. I owed everything to him."

*Sarah (Cissie) Stewart, Great Britain, Freestyle Swimmer 1928 Olympics.*

"I was the youngest of seven children, and my father was keen on sports. He played football for Newton Heath who are called Manchester United now. My father encouraged my swimming, but things were different then. There were no sponsors, no going to a warm country to train, no electronic timing, everything was timed by hand held watches. I worked hard on my own to get where I did. My training was hard going - I just swam up and down. I never had a coach, I just used to watch my older sister, Margaret - she was a champion - and try to do the same, length after length. I was also working in a baker's shop and I had to wash the windows at half past six in the morning  before anyone else came in, and I got off at five o'clock. When I was training seriously I used to go down to the baths twice a day and swim 30 lengths. That's all I did.

One time when it was coming up to the Olympics I remember going to the pool twice a day. This particular day the baths manager took me to one side and reprimanded me for using my season ticket twice in the same day! I was accused of trying to cheat the rate-payers and had to buy a series of additional tickets to complete my training.

When I saw the pool at the Olympic trials in Blackpool, I'll never forget the size of it, I'd never seen anything like it in my life. I'd never swum in a pool longer than 22 yards! I thought, oh, do I have to swim to the very end?"
(Cissie was the Scottish 880 yards record holder at the time!)

### Pat Norton, Australia, Backstroke Swimmer 1936 Olympics.

"I believe our fates are mapped out for us. The fate of my swimming career was made long before I was born. My mother was a nurse in a country town in 1916 and became friends with a family whose son she had cared for, but time and distance separated them. Fourteen years later, when I was twelve, by a chance reconciliation I met the young patient, now a grown man and he became my swimming coach."

*Pat Norton (PD)*

It has always been important for young sporting hopefuls to find support and encouragement from families and mentors. Yet how much more vital was that support from fathers, schoolteachers and coaches for young women like these. It is impossible to imagine how many other young women missed their chance in the early days of the modern Olympics simply because they were unfortunate enough to be born into the wrong environment.

Throughout the pre-war years, the dice were to be loaded against women at the Olympics, partly because the one man who might have encouraged their participation - the founder of the modern Games - was set firmly against it.

# CHAPTER FOUR
## One Step Forward, Two Steps Back: 1904-1924

Baron Pierre de Coubertin, the 'father' of the modern Olympic Games, did not move with the times or change his views on women and Olympism. He found it impossible during his twenty-six years of IOC leadership to encourage women or promote women's events and would never have dreamed of them becoming IOC members. Coubertin died in 1937 and to the end he believed that the ideal woman was one who produced male athletes - not one who was athletic herself. He did, however, approve of *one* medal that was awarded to a woman. Writing about the Stockholm Olympics of 1912, he said:

> "A Swedish woman, Madame Wersall, had six sons engaged in the Games, the younger ones in the role of boy scouts registered to aid in keeping order and as messengers. Is this not antique (in keeping with the spirit of the Greek Games)? The International Olympic Committee has awarded her the Olympic medal." [1]

**Good Guys 1**
**Justinien de Clary (IOC Member) in the IOC session at the Salle de Leys, City Hall Antwerp, 1920:**
> 'The strong women make our mankind strong and there are many women who can compete with us men already.'

Perhaps because of Coubertin's and many of the IOC's continuing intransigence, it proved extremely difficult for any sports for women to win permanent acceptance as part of the official programme during the early years of the Games. The female foot was wedged firmly in the Olympic door, but quite what that foot had on it - tennis pumps, runners' spikes, or golfing shoes - changed year by year.

## Women's Events Come and Go in the Olympic Games

Many sports strive to become recognised as Olympic, and, as a result, some have been included at the Games as exhibitions or demonstrations, whilst not actually forming part of the competition proper. Some have gone on to be permanent parts of the Olympic programme whilst others have had to wait. The years before the Second World War saw many changes of the events in which women were allowed to compete.

## St Louis, 1904 - the New Amazons

By 1904, it had been decided to withdraw the right for women to participate in the two events in which they had 'officially' competed in 1900 - tennis and golf. The only official sport for women at the St Louis Games was archery - but only American competitors took part. There was one other unusual event for women - an exhibition of women's boxing! It is said the fights generated into bloody conflicts egged on by the cheering crowds, and it never appeared again.

It was perhaps not surprising that archery should get its turn on the Olympic programme for women. It had long been seen as a suitable activity for a lady - it was not too energetic and drawing a bow was regarded as graceful, feminine and dignified. It has been called a noble art: "... well becoming, ev'n in the softer sex."[1] In Greek legend, a race of female warriors called Amazons were said to have cut off their right breast to draw the bow more easily, a practice modern female archers fortunately have not felt compelled to follow.

**Queen Elizabeth I was a keen archer and appointed a Royal Commission to supervise the care of the bow.**

In medieval England, skills with a bow were practised on every village green and the bow had been the weapon of ordinary folk well before archery became a sport and leisure activity for the gentry.

In the late 17th century, the Prince Regent gave archery his blessing as an acceptable pastime for young 'Bucks' and it became an important part of the social round. Clubs were formed, including in 1781 the Toxophilite Society, the archers' governing body. Most were male dominated, with women's archery treated as a lavish side entertainment rather than a proper sporting event, but three clubs admitted women. The Royal British Bowmen, in spite of their name, were very much a 'mixed' society and were the first to become so in 1787. There is evidence that this club was formed on the instigation of a woman, Lady Cunliffe. Wildly enthusiastic after receiving instruction in archery, she persuaded her reluctant husband, Sir Foster Cunliffe, to take it up himself and to form the society.

**A petticoat was the name given in 1803 to the piece of cloth on the target face which shows after the outer line is painted. It is still called this today.**

The competitive nature of women's archery was firmly established in 1845 when eight women competed for the first National Championship.

The 1845 rules for women stated:

> "For Ladies, the number of arrows each day shall be four dozen at 60 yards, and if both days be wet the number shall be two dozen. The ground for the Ladies shall be open after Luncheon..." [2]

Queen Victoria was patron of one of the early archery clubs, the Queen's Royal St. Leonard's Archers, and the young princess shot with them before her accession to the throne. Her Majesty often presented annual prizes and the St. Leonard's round included an extra three arrows tacked on the end of a standard round because she had once arrived late!

Many more clubs were formed by women but there was some opposition. Some people thought that "...in a short space of time a most fragile young woman, by means of judicious archery practice would develop muscles that when her arms were flexed, rolled up into balls like a blacksmith's biceps."3 Fortunately women ignored this advice - perhaps because archery had other compensations, such as allowing them to socialise with eligible bachelors. There was also money to be made in competing. Prizes could be lavish, and many a widow engaged in archery competition to supplement a meagre income.

> **Women archers are still known as 'Lasses of the Forest'.**

The most famous and skilful female archer in Great Britain was Alice B. Legh who became Lady Champion Archer twenty three times between 1881 and 1922.

She would have been in a strong position to win at the St Louis Olympics in 1904, but Great Britain sent no archery team, and the American Lydia Scott Howell (a mere *seventeen* times American Lady Champion) won the gold medal in both the Double National and Columbia Round.

In spite of the opportunities archery offered for courtship, Alice never married. Unusually for this period, she also wrote in the *'Archery'* (a publication of the time) on the benefits of the sport for ladies. This charted new territory - a woman writing as an expert in a mixed sport. In her opinion,

> *"For delicate and growing girls archery is a most healthy exercise, taking them out into the fresh air...and most suitable to the matron who feels it undignified to take part in some outdoor games and yet is quite young enough to enjoy them."* 4

*Queenie Newall (GB), Olympic Archery Champion 1908 (HS)*

In 1908 in the London Olympics archery entries were still low with only 25 British competitors shooting against each other, the hoped-for French female contingent having failed to turn up at the last moment. In inclement weather, amidst empty spectator stands, the gold medal in the Double National round was won by Queenie Newall with Lottie Dod of Wimbledon tennis fame getting the silver. Alice had been invited to take part in the Games, but Queenie was her protégée, and she may have stood aside to let her win the glory.

It may have been that Alice was preparing to defend her title at the National Championships, scheduled shortly after the Olympics, where there was always a big following, and she may have considered this more meritorious. Another possibility is that the strongly competitive Alice considered Queenie a threat; but at any rate Queenie was Champion at the age of fifty-three, and remains the oldest woman to win an Olympic gold medal. After 1908 archery was dropped from the Olympic programme until 1972, although men competed in 1920 in Antwerp.

## Swimming

Swimming for men was one of the first Olympic sports in 1896, but women had to wait a few more years. Sweden's Miss Ebba Gisico along with women swimmers from Iceland, gave popular displays of swimming and diving in 1908 in the London Olympics. This led to the first competitive swimming and diving in 1912 at the Stockholm Games with just one individual swimming event, the 100 metres freestyle, the team relay and highboard diving. Like many sports, swimming had been thought unladylike and too physically demanding, and the limited women's programme reflected this.

Evelyn de Lacy, Australia, Freestyle swimmer 1936.
"I was one of eleven children and learned to swim in the Swan River. Girls weren't allowed to swim in what was called 'swim throughs' before they were fourteen as it was considered too hard for them. By the time I was fifteen I was the Australian freestyle champion. In Western Australia we did all our swimming in the river. The pools were built on the river, with floating pontoons for turning boards to cope with the fall of the tide.

I had my first coach Jack Sheedy, secretary of the Swimming Association, when I was turned sixteen. We had to pay our own way to the Berlin Games (1936), but a newspaper came to my aid and paid my fare."

We will never know for certain how our ancestors developed their swimming techniques and water skills. We can look at art work and vases and go back to pre-historic civilisations to see that where there was water there was swimming, for survival and for fun. Women and girls in Ancient Egypt bathed in the river Nile and - like Evelyn de Lacy many centuries later - soon learned to swim.

During the Dark Ages in Europe, swimming was most unpopular and water was thought to spread disease. It was not until the eighteenth century that bathing was taken up without fear and alarm. The revival began in England, where spas and baths were established to rival swimming in lakes, rivers and sea, and swimming and mixed bathing became popular again. Sea bathing became fashionable towards the end of the eighteenth century when its benefits for health were much vaunted.

Competitive swimming began in earnest in the nineteenth century, with the growth of purpose-built baths where contests and galas were held. The first swimming clubs were established in the 1860s and inter-club competition soon followed. Women in England established their own separate swimming clubs as early as 1884, and pools exclusively for women were also built. When the English Amateur Swimming Association was formed in 1886 it enforced a strict amateur code and regulations, and the less desirable elements of the sport, betting and unruliness, were eliminated.

_____*Fascinating Aquatic Females 1*_____

*Minna Wookey*

**In July 1885, a bet for a gold medal was accepted by a Mr Wookey who was asked to find anyone who could swim half a mile in the River Avon with hands and feet tied. He accepted the bet on behalf of his eleven year old daughter, Minna. On Friday July 24th, the committee of the Leander Swimming Club and members of the press took a boat on the river to adjudicate the event. The young swimmer was tied up and in she dived! 20,000 people turned up to watch her effort. With encouragement from her father and support from the cheering crowds, Minna Wookey completed the swim.**

During the nineteenth century, nude bathing had been common place, but concerns increased about decency and respectability. It was thought that the sight of a naked body would lead inevitably to lust and carnal desires, so people began to cover themselves up. By 1900, a debate arose about whether or not men and women should even swim together and mixed bathing was banned at many pools. Women's costumes became incredibly restrictive - thick, sometimes woollen knickerbockers to the knee and tunics belted at the waist were common place. In Great Britain, the 1909 Costume Law said that, "Drawers under the costume must be of triangular pattern, with a minimum width of two and a half inches at the fork; they must meet on each hip and must not be less than 3 inches on each side when fastened."[1]

These garments were vital to maintain decency and respectability - but not helpful if you wanted to swim very fast. The Amateur Swimming Association of

Great Britain introduced detailed regulations about swimming costumes. The issue of clothing was to have repercussions for many female swimmers.

_____ *Fascinating Aquatic Females 2* _____

*Annette Kellerman*

**Australia's Annette Kellerman had taken up swimming as therapy to strengthen her weak legs. In the early 1900s, she began to win awards at local swimming galas, and became New South Wales' champion at the hundred yards, one mile and long-distance swim. Annette began to recognise her talent as a swimmer but, as the opportunities for her to demonstrate her skills were restricted and Olympic competition was not open to women at this time, she went into show business and gave swimming and diving demonstrations. There was a lot of interest in long-distance swimming and Annette came to Europe and tried to swim the Channel. Although she failed, she became famous and began to design swimming costumes, frustrated at being handicapped by the skirted bathing suit. She swam Boston Harbour wearing an 'indecent' one-piece bathing suit, and was arrested for exposing her legs. Undeterred, she invented the two-piece for women - an early bikini. Annette Kellerman was born too soon for Olympic swimming but by her example she encouraged women to take up sport for fitness and was a keen advocate of women's rights.**

The first woman to swim the English Channel was Gertrude Ederle(USA)in 1926 in a time of 14 hours and 34 minutes. In the 1924 Olympics Gertrude won a bronze medal in 100 metres freestyle and a gold in the relay.

By 1912, when women's swimming first appeared on the Olympic programme, there was opposition to sending women swimmers to the Stockholm Olympic Games from both America and Australia, though for different reasons. The American Olympic Committee was opposed to women participating in events where they couldn't wear long skirts. They thought swimming would foster immodesty and immorality and that bloomers were unacceptable. The American women stuck together and their women tennis players walked out in sympathy - so the Olympic Committee left all the women behind!

For the Australians, it was a question not so much of modesty as of cost. The Australians had a swimmer, Sarah 'Fanny' Durack, who held the world record for the 100 metres

*Fanny Durack (gold, Australia), Mina Wylie (silver, Australia) and Jennie Fletcher (bronze, GB) 1912 (IG)*

freestyle but they were initially fiercely opposed to sending her to the Olympics. Australian sport at this time was very male-oriented. After months of debate, the Australian Olympic Council eventually voted to allow women to compete.

*1912 British relay team and chaperone (IG)*

However, neither the Australian government nor the Council would agree to finance their two swimmers, Durack and Wilhelmina (Mina) Wylie. Fanny and Mina had to fund their own journey to the games - a considerable expense at that time.

Competing in the 100 metres freestyle in an acceptable long woollen swimsuit and skirt, Fanny won gold in 1:22.2 and became the first woman Olympic swimming champion. Her winning time was exactly the same as that of Alfred Hajos when he won the men's event in 1896.

Fanny and Mina became the first Australian women to compete at the Olympics in 1912. In winning gold and silver, half the Australian team's medal tally, their success could not be ignored by the Australian Council. Fanny and Mina's single-mindedness and determination to compete at the Olympics is an important landmark in Australian women's sporting history.

At the 1912 Stockholm Games, Jennie Fletcher of Great Britain took the bronze medal behind Fanny and Mina and the first relay gold went to Great Britain. Meanwhile, the 1908 Scandinavian diving exhibition in London had inspired two Swedish highdivers to seek glory. Greta Johanson and Lisa Regnell won gold and silver, with Britain's Isabella White taking bronze.

> **Swimming Notes October 1885**
> "We trust the time is not far distant when every board school will possess a swimming bath for girls and boys, and half an hour's bathing each morning would add very much to the virtue of the girls and the honour and bravery of the boys." [2]

*Jennie Fletcher (Great Britain) 1912 (IG)*

*Bella White (Great Britain) competed 1912-28 and won bronze in 1912 (IG)*

### Signe Johansson, Sweden, Diver 1924

"In a small town in Sweden they had a swimming competition. I was the only girl, but won over all the boys and went home with twelve silver spoons which was first prize. In December 1923 Eric Bergvall, who was head of Stockholm Stadium and chairman of the Swedish Swimming Association, asked us three girls in Stockholm if we wanted to try springdive for the upcoming Olympics in Paris 1924. We were glad and excited and said 'Yes! Of course!' Diving in the 1920s consisted of a standing jump from a diving board, five and ten metres, standing and with advance. A dry dive construction was built in a room at Stockholm Stadium existing of a springboard, lots of sawdust and a belt for the person who was training. We often trained with our male friends who were all top gymnasts and taught us a lot. There was not much practice in water."

The 1924 games, held in Paris, are the furthest back in time we have been able to go for first hand memories. Dutch swimmer Marie Vierdag, Swedish diver Signe Johansson and American diver Carol Fletcher were there.

*1924 USA Women's Olympic swimming and diving team (CM)*

Signe:

*"We were promised we would travel to Paris two weeks before the competitions and practise in their new and modern swimming bath. All said and done, we were in Paris two weeks in advance but we were extremely surprised when the pool had no water in it! Instead we spent our days in Paris sightseeing and improving our French! I was very glad that I qualified for the final but also very disappointed when I missed my last jump. You cannot do that. I reckon I could have done better than fifth place if my last jump had been better, but I didn't have a chance to take gold or silver as the top girls had competed in the previous Olympic Games, and they also had a long time of practice behind them."*

Fellow diver Carol Fletcher, the American, travelled from Pasadena to New York to travel by sea to the Paris Olympics. Speaking in Santa Barbara in 1996, aged 89, she told the crowd that she was very pleased that there were more men than women on the ship!

*Diver Carol Fletcher (USA) 1924 (CM)*

Like Signe, Marie Vierdag's experiences of the Paris games were mixed:

> *"In the 400 metres I earned one point for my country. The Games were badly organised. We had a bad hotel, dirty, and bad food. I remember my first race. I was eighteen, I was ready to start, and the starter said to me was I wearing a skirt under my costume - and of course I wasn't. I had to go back and find one. Every one else was wearing one, but I didn't know you had to have one.*

> *They entered me in the 400 metres freestyle but I couldn't swim all the way doing the crawl at that time as it was too much for me. I hadn't learnt crawl properly then, so I swam scissors legs and sidestroke arms for the first two hundred and crawl for the last two hundred!"*

Such was the attitude of the trainers and organisers to women's participation that Marie had not realised that she was improperly attired for her first Olympic race, and was even entered for an event in a stroke that she hadn't trained for! This 'have-a-go' approach to Olympic competition was typical and was to have major repercussions for women's athletics at a later time. Marie went on to compete for Holland in a further two Olympics, including Los Angeles in 1932 where she won a bronze in the relay. But it was particularly special to swim on home territory in 1928 when the Olympics came to Holland, as we shall hear in a later chapter. By then, women's swimming would have truly arrived at the Olympic Games.

*Marie Vierdag in 1922 in all her finery (MS)*

## Gymnastics

While swimming was well on the way to full acceptance as an Olympic sport for women, the gymnasts were having a tougher time. A bid for women's gymnastics to be considered appeared as early as 1906, when a group of sixteen gymnasts from Denmark performed at the King's invitation in a demonstration at the Interim Games in Greece. This was followed in 1908 by a second exhibition at the London Games, where women's gymnastic teams from Norway, Sweden, Denmark and Great Britain were well received. The London Daily Telegraph of July 14th 1908 wrote: "The ladies who took part lent to the exhibition a grace and charm all their own."[1] The displays by twenty or more Danish gymnasts, who competed in white serge gymnastic costumes, pale brown stockings and without shoes were particularly popular.

It was the ancient Greeks who gave us the word gymnastics. It had been one of the oldest Olympic sports, practised also by the early civilisations of China, Egypt and Iran. In the Palace of Knossos in Crete, the discovery of a cave painting of a female acrobat vaulting over the horns of a bull reveals that gymnastics was also a very early and very daring sport for women. Leaping over a running bull demanded physical ability, precision of movement, practice and courage on the part of the leaper, who grasped the horns and turned a somersault in the air before landing. The bull was a somewhat lethal forerunner of the vaulting horse that is used in Olympic gymnastics today.

**Women competed on the swinging rings in the German gymnasia in the 1870s and parallel bars in the 1920s and 30s.**

The resurgence of gymnastics in Europe came in the eighteenth century with the development of Swedish and German gymnastic systems, designed to improve the health of young people. Dr. Ling's Swedish system was originally intended as a form of medical treatment but practitioners took it to other countries to encourage the proper development of children. When Madame Bergman-Österberg, a Swedish physical training expert, came to London to introduce the 'Ling' system she also founded the first College of Physical Education for Girls in 1885. Regulation knickerbockers and long black stockings came into their own for gymnastics in schools, providing girls with the freedom to perform exercises in comfort. So that they could enjoy the pleasures and benefits of physical activity without any restrictions Madame Österberg did something quite revolutionary - she refused to allow her students to wear corsets and hats during exercise!

Military instructors were often chosen for drill instruction and army sergeants who instructed in boys' schools were also employed in girls'. At Bedford High School, England, in 1883 the girls found their former army sergeant "rather a dragon and very impatient with us."2

Fortunately for the girls, Madame Österberg became a visiting 'drill mistress' in place of the sergeant, and her assistant, Miss Stansfeld, founded another Physical Training College in the town.

In the 1890s, the Board of Education in Great Britain provided money for physical training and drill in schools and gymnastics was readily taken up as a suitable activity for both girls and boys. A Drill Guide Book of 1894 for teachers advises 'When mixed classes of boys and girls are exercising, the girls should refrain

*Girls at Bedford High School using ropes, late 1890's (BHS)*

from performing certain exercises.'3 It is unclear whether the concern was for modesty and decorum or the effect that exercise might have on the girls' reproductive capacity, but it is likely that it was for both - though what is meant by the 'certain exercises' referred to seemed to rest entirely on the discretion of the teacher.

*Bedford High School gymnastics 1915 (BHS)*

In schools without gymnasia, with no playground or during inclement weather, drill was modified and exercises were performed in the class room at desks. This became known as 'desk drill gymnastics'. Interest grew amongst the working class and girls' gymnastic clubs developed, making gymnastics the first sport for women to evolve from populist roots rather than amongst the leisured and moneyed classes.

The first 'women only' gymnasia had been opened in Paris in 1829 and in Eiselen, Germany, in 1832. By the end of the nineteenth century gymnastics became so fashionable that clubs were set up throughout Europe.

*Poise and elegance at Bedford High School 1915 (BHS)*

With the formation of the International Gymnastics Federation in 1881 and the National Governing Body of Gymnastics in London in 1888, international competition became possible.

In the Olympic Games in Sweden in 1912 there was still no competition for women, but there was a third and even more impressive exhibition given by Norway, Finland, Sweden and Denmark, who fielded a huge team of one hundred and forty eight gymnasts. 'Feminine' gymnastic displays, it seemed, were perfectly acceptable - it was competitiveness and shows of strength that got women into trouble.

The outbreak of the First World War prevented further gymnastic developments. There was little support for women in gymnastic federations and few women had any experience in developing or organising their own sport. In 1924 when Great Britain held its first women's National Championship it was viewed with suspicion.

*Carrie Pickles (GB) joyfully contorting in 1928 (GL)*

There was disapproval in some quarters from those who preferred women gymnasts not to be competing or venturing into male sports, and the women gymnasts even had to assure the press that they suffered no ill effects from their strenuous exertions. The British women were described by a number of male British critics as 'brazen hussies' for 'contorting their bodies in a way that God had not intended.'4 Eventually, in 1928, the International Olympic Committee approved a women's team gymnastic competition with, most importantly, a women's jury to judge the event - this development was indeed progress, and would lead to women coaching and managing their own teams.

But the International Federation of Gymnastics did not organise a women's competition in Los Angeles at the Olympic Games of 1932, nor were there any of the popular exhibitions. The depression, the low priority of women's gymnastics in America and the distances European women would have had to travel were all contributory factors. When the Games returned to Europe in 1936, gymnastics came with them and the sport has remained in the Olympic programme ever since, with the inclusion of the individual competition in 1952 .

# Fencing

Baron de Coubertin was himself a fencer, and fencing was one of the original events in the 1896 Olympics for men. Women had already made great headway in this apparently war-like sport, yet until 1924 the world's greatest women fencers were unable to compete in the Olympic Games.

In order to survive it had been necessary to 'master' the sword in almost all parts of the world. The Bronze and Iron Ages saw the evolution of daggers and swords, while the knights of the Middle Ages favoured a heavy two-handed broadsword which could pierce heavy armour. When gunpowder was invented in the 1500s and armour became redundant, the sword changed yet again and the fashion was for something lighter and more manageable. Without armour, swordsmanship was even more important, and fencing schools and fencing masters began to appear to coach the skills. Masters, vying for supremacy, guarded their teaching secrets and fencing became a highly secretive art.

During Louis XIV's reign, books appeared in France about fencing and the French developed a style with a short, light court sword from which the fencing sword called the épée developed. Eventually what had formerly been a deadly method of combat became a recognised sport - one in which, despite its combative nature, women could compete. Around 1800, more protective rules were adopted, and with the appearance of the wire-mesh mask modern fencing emerged.

The first fencing associations were created towards the end of the 19th century throughout Europe and many European women began to take part. Fencing was found to be a good form of exercise which could be pursued equally well in all weathers, places and seasons. It required no cumbersome and time-consuming preparation of nets, marking of courts, erecting of goal posts or engaging of caddies, and so it became ever more popular amongst the leisured classes. A growing number of women's competitions developed and at the end of the nineteenth century women's fencing was of a particularly high standard.

*Toupie Lowther in 1900 (MF)*

*Toupie Lowther*

In Great Britain, a female fencer, Miss Toupie Lowther, was described in the press in 1898 as 'better than most men' and 'the best lady fencer with the foil in the world'. The same year Toupie caused a furore when, in an interview in the London Daily Mail, she announced that compared to French fencers, no-one in England really knew how to fence! This caused an uproar in the fencing world and an exchange of letters in the Daily Mail in which an anonymous correspondent, 'Sixte', wrote: "Is Miss Lowther really serious when she affirms that no one in England knows how to fence? It appears to be a somewhat sweeping assertion when such a man as Captain Alfred Hutton still walks this planet, to say nothing of several other leading exponents who I venture could teach even so redoubtable a person as Miss Lowther a few points in either the Italian or French styles."

*Toupie Lowther fencing M. Ridderbaeks (MF)*

Toupie's father, Captain Lowther, in response and on her behalf, challenged Captain Hutton or any English gentleman to a fencing contest, the loser to pay fifty pounds to the Prince of Wales Hospital Fund. The episode was drawn to a conclusion when Captain Hutton himself wrote that it was an impertinence to himself and the young lady, and further suggested that the meeting for a wager would disqualify both as amateurs if such a contest took place. The final word went to a French fencer, 'Cyrano', who said that he was astonished that a friendly challenge was met with no acceptance in England, while in France the spirit of courtesy would bring forward three hundred candidates who would gladly pick up the gauntlet!

. . SECOND . .

**GRAND ASSAULT-AT-ARMS,**

— Sabre, Foil, and Duelling Sword (Exhibition) —

International Competition for Ladies, and also for Gentlemen.

FOR THE PROMOTION OF FENCING IN ENGLAND.

AT THE

**EMPRESS ROOMS**

**Royal Palace Hotel,**
KENSINGTON, W.

Saturday, 20th February, 1904,
At **9** p.m.

*Poster for a Grand Assault-At-Arms 1904 (MF)*

How she would have fared against Captain Hutton will never be known, but because of her ability and skill Toupie Lowther regularly fought, and defeated, male fencers. Yet the Olympic stage was denied her presence. Toupie Lowther had strong views about the benefits fencing had for women, and, when questioned about the possibility of women sustaining injuries from fencing said:

> *"Injurious? Certainly not! It ought to be considered a necessary part of every girl's education. It is not half so dangerous as either gymnastics or cycling. Once a woman really takes to fencing she does not drop it again as she might drop tennis or golf or cycling."[1]*

Toupie Lowther may never have competed at any Olympic Games but she does deserve a footnote in Olympic history quite separate from her pioneering fencing. Toupie defeated Charlotte Cooper in tennis - just two months before Charlotte became the very first individual woman Olympic gold medalist.

The eminent fencers of the time did their best to publicise and promote fencing for women but they could only set the seed. In 1924, at the first Olympics in which fencing appeared in

*1924 British Women's Olympic fencers, from left: Gladys Davis, Alice Walker, Gladys Daniell and Muriel Freeman (MF)*

the programme for women, Ellen Ossier of Denmark won the gold medal, Gladys Davis, Great Britain, the silver and Greta Heckscher, also of Denmark, the bronze in the individual foil competition.

Fencing has remained an Olympic sport for women since its introduction in 1924, and the team foil competition was introduced in 1960.

_____ *Formidable Female Fencers 2* _____

*Kerstin Palm*

**Kerstin Palm, Swedish fencer, was the first Olympian to take part in seven Olympics, from 1964-88 - the most achieved by any fencer and any woman, in any sport.**

**"I have quite a lot of sad and tragic memories from the Olympic Games but also many nice and happy ones, among them being the only**

woman in the world to take part in so many Olympic Games. People often ask me which of the Games I remember best but I can never really say because every Olympic city and organisation has made their organisation so unique that it cannot possibly be compared with another.

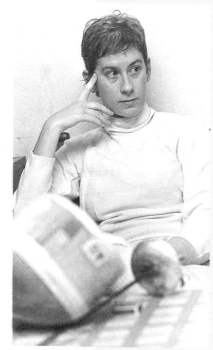

*Kerstin Palm (KP)*

There have been many changes in fencing since I began in my first Olympic Games in 1964. Many fencers nowadays are more or less professionals. The equipment has changed a lot and become better and more secure, and therefore thicker and heavier. Among the best male fencers it is not any more possible to combine fencing in two or three weapons if you want to reach world class, but exceptionally it happened in the sixties.

I can't say that I have a ranking list among the best Olympic fencers in the world because I haven't seen the perfect fencer yet. I never will - but of course I have seen a lot of splendid fencers. Most of them are from East Europe because there they always had such a high technical standard in their training. These countries are Hungary, Poland, Romania and the former **USSR**. Maybe the best technical fencers ever seen come from France. Italy also produced many excellent fencers. Because of tradition women only fenced foil in the Olympic Games and other championships for a long time, but now it changes slowly but surely. Nowadays épée fencing for women is a part of the Olympic programme, and this year sabre fencing for women will also be a part of the world championship programme, but not yet accepted in the Olympic Games. It will probably come in the future!

One of my most important memories was at Munich in 1972. I arrived at the Olympic Village as soon as it opened, and therefore I got a room at one end of the female village close to the fence and just a few yards from the rest of the village. On the same day the Israeli fencing team arrived, and these boys got their rooms very close to mine but on the other side of the fence. In the training hall I had many opportunities to train with them, and I even got a lesson from their coach, and we became very good friends.

One night when the Games had started I woke up because there was a terrible noise outside my house on the other side of the fence and I heard glass being smashed. After a while everything became absolutely quiet again and I fell asleep without thinking of it any more. Next morning we all realised what had happened. Palestinian terrorists had entered the Israeli house through the windows and shot Israeli competitors, among others one of the fencers and also the fencing coach. So two of my friends were murdered just a few yards from me, I didn't understand anything until ten hours later. These seconds of terror have been in my thoughts year after year more than anything else except my competitions in my seven Olympic Games.

I have participated in seven Olympic Games but sadly because of an injury to my hip joint I no longer compete, so I will not be competing in Sydney. In fact I have little to do with fencing today. I retired in 1991 after thirty years of active foil fencing. Since 1970 I have been working as a dentist and have my own private practise in central Stockholm. A few years ago I donated my complete trophy collection to the Sport Museum of Göthenburg, the city where I started fencing. It consisted of several thousand items weighing over 300 kilograms."

By the 1920s, women had made considerable strides in forging a place for themselves at the Games. Swimming was firmly established as an Olympic sport, women fencers were on the verge of success and even the gymnasts were hopeful their battle would be won in the end. Though question marks still stood over individual sports, there no longer seemed to be any doubt about women's participation in the Olympics.

But there was one crucial field where women had yet to prove themselves at Olympic level - athletics. The journey to full acceptance for women athletes was only just beginning and, like Stamata Revithi's marathon run, it was to prove no easy road.

## CHAPTER FIVE - The Biggest Hurdle:
## Women Athletes' Fight to Win a Place at The Olympic Games

By the end of the nineteenth century, women and girls had already shown that they could take part in energetic sports and race walking, yet could still bear children and do the expected heavy household tasks. As we have seen, women showing muscle, sweating, puffing or running was particularly alarming to our Victorian forebears, so those who fought for women's athletics to be included in the Olympic Games faced even greater

*Field Day, 1899. An early high jump competition with hands on the bar (VCR)*

opposition. Genteel women had served overhead in tennis, but throwing a javelin was seen as a different matter, and many people were opposed to it.

### Gertrude Wilhelmsen, USA, Javelin and Discus 1936 Olympics.

"Mother died in a flu epidemic, so we children stayed with different relatives until we were old enough to live with father and help out on the farm. Father was a farmer raising hops and vegetables. Sports were unheard of at that time for people struggling to make a living.

I first became interested in sports in the first grade, when I could beat the boys in races. The track meets between schools showed up my competitive spirit. I'll never forget my embarrassment when my garter holding up my black stockings broke and I had to take hold with my hand to finish the race - and I won first place. That was the start of my career!

At high school I broke the National High School record in javelin, 103 feet 10 inches. The coach had a record book in her pocket and checked it out. As soon as we got back to the gym word got round and immediately the bell rang that meant a special assembly for honouring me, and they all hooted and hollered 'Hooray for Gertie!'

**My training was done at the school's athletics field, sometimes at the same time as the boys practised. My coach, Pop Logan, helped both the boys and the girls. He influenced me to try out for the Olympics."**

The earliest modern records of women's athletics events go back to 9th November 1895 at Vassar College, a private college for women in Poughkeepsie, New York State. Soon Austrian, Swedish, Canadian, French, British, Russian and Finnish women all had athletics results officially recorded and recognised before the outbreak of World War I in 1914.

In Europe, a most significant development occurred in France in 1917 when three women's athletics clubs formed the Federation Feminine Sportive de France and held the first French athletics championships for women. Other European countries soon followed with their own championships - Austria in 1918, Belgium, Czechoslovakia, Finland, Germany, and Netherlands all in 1921. In Britain women had competed officially in teams for the women's services in 1919, and three years later, in 1922, the English Women's Amateur Athletic Association (WAAA) was formed.

**Princess Mary asked that the 1908 marathon race start under the nursery window of Windsor Castle so that her children could watch! The start was moved back and so the distance of the marathon became 26 miles and 385 yards but no woman was allowed to run it.**

For international competition to become established, it often requires a presiding genius - in this case a remarkable Frenchwoman, in many ways women's answer to Olympic founder Baron Pierre de Coubertin.

## Alice Milliat

In 1919, Alice Milliat, one of the founders of the French women's federation, approached the International Olympic Committee to include women's athletics in the 1920 Olympic Games. She was unsuccessful, but undeterred Alice set out to find another way to achieve her goals - something quite remarkable for the times. Throughout history, women who have had difficulty penetrating men's institutions have taken a separatist line and set up their own competing organisations. Alice Milliat was remarkable in deciding to do it on a world scale. Between 1921 and 1936, she was instrumental in developing the Federation Sportive Feminine International (FSFI).

Initially this involved just six countries - France, USA, Britain, Czechoslovakia, Italy and Switzerland, but it was to become the main women's athletics body and the driving force behind early international athletics for women. Alice Milliat, who was supported in the early days by three French athletes - Suzanne Liebrard, Germaine Delapierre and Therese Brule - became the President of the FSFI.

Their dogged belief that women's athletics were important led to the first international women's competition which was held in Monte Carlo in 1921, with five nations, France, Italy, Norway, Switzerland and Great Britain competing. The

participants called these games 'Les Premiéres Olympiades de Monte Carlo' - a cheeky gesture designed to make the men take notice.

The star of these games was British athlete Mary Lines who had never run a race until she was twenty-seven. At the games, Mary took three individual first places (60 metres, 250 metres and long jump), was second in the 800 metres, and had a place in the winning relay team.

*Drill at the 1921 Monte Carlo Women's World Games (PHM)*

The Monte Carlo Games included a number of other sports for women and Mary also played for the winning basketball team!

## Good Guys 2
**Camille Blanc (Mayor of Beaulieu and President of the International Sporting Club of Monaco)** - *sent out invitations and made the Monte Carlo venue available for the first women's International Games of 1921 and 1922.*

At the second women's international athletics event in 1922, also held in Monte Carlo, there was an increase in competing countries to seven, with Czecho-Slovakia and Belgium now competing. The second congress of the FSFI, in 1922, ratified the women's world records and voted to hold a Women's Olympic Games in Paris in August 1922. Women's athletics was going forward!

More than thirty thousand spectators watched the march-past of competing nations at the Pershing Stadium in Paris on Sunday August 20th, 1922 when Alice Milliat spoke the words:
*"Je proclaime ouverts les premiers Jeux Olympiques Féminins du Monde."*
*(I declare open the first Women's Olympic Games of the World.)*

With these simple words, the remarkable Alice Milliat threw down the gauntlet. Now the men would have to pay attention.

At this time, athletics for women was so new that the rules of competition and definitions of amateurism had to be agreed. Vera Searle Palmer, British international athlete in the 1920s and co-founder of the English Women's Amateur Athletics Association, said that the WAAA had simply used the men's rule book as their own, making small changes like 'him' to 'her'. The task of inaugurating women's athletics internationals, co-ordinating the rules of the many governing bodies, as well as challenging the negative attitudes of the time is worth a posthumous acknowledgement for Alice Milliat. Avery Brundage, President of the IOC 1952-1972, said of her: "She was active for years and years and she demanded more and more. She made quite a nuisance of herself." [1]

As many women have found, being a nuisance works. At the First Olympic Games for Women in Paris, sixty five participants from five countries set eighteen world records in the eleven competitions, and the Games were a huge success. This success showed that there was significant interest in women's athletics (as Alice Milliat and her supporters had always known) and so the FSFI decided to expand further and to hold the Games every four years, like the men. Now opposition began to stir itself, as it became clear that the women might be on the verge of stealing the men's thunder.

The IOC called this development "abuse and excess" [2] and in 1923 suggested that the International Amateur Athletics Federation (IAAF) should address the problem. Many men's athletics clubs had begun to include events for women so the issues raised certainly needed addressing but when the women renewed their application to compete in athletics in the official 1924 Olympics it was *again* rejected. It was as if there were a tacit agreement to block Alice Milliat at every turn. The IAAF voted that same year to be responsible for women's athletics but still took the view that women should not be allowed into athletics events at the Olympic Games.

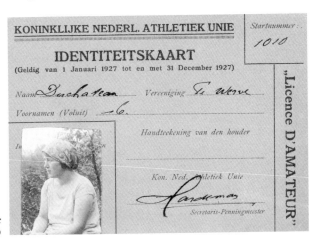

Mien Duchateau's (Holland) amateur athletic license of 1927 (BVD)

Matilde Moraschi (100 metres) and Vittorina Vivenza (Discus), Italy, 1928 Olympics.

"I was 16 when my brother showed me a photograph of a sports ground in a sports paper in which there were girls wearing t-shirts and shorts who were racing. As I was a bit of a tom boy, I went to have a look and immediately enrolled in the club 'Forza Coraggio' (Strength and Courage)." (Matilde)

"I became an athlete as a result of taking part in a race at school when my female PE teacher noticed I ran well, so I started training. In Aosta in 1924, there were no sports grounds or clubs and I would train in the military square with the soldiers." (Vittorina)

The FSFI protested at the lack of support until a compromise was worked out which enabled the women to remain independent. They continued to use the IAAF's rules and regulations but organised their own events.

A tiny chink of Olympic opportunity opened. A twelve-person 'Olympic Committee for Women's Sports' was appointed to report on the possible staging of women's events at the next Olympic Games in Amsterdam. Meanwhile, the IOC insisted that the next Women's World Games (planned for 1926 in Göthenburg Sweden) were not to be called 'Olympic' as they had sole right to the title.

*Vittorina Vivenza (Italy) (VVD)*

*Matilde Moraschi (Italy) (MM)*

Eventually the IAAF suggested that women were admitted as a trial in the Amsterdam Olympics of 1928 but in a limited programme of five events only. As a result Alice Milliat spiritedly said:

*"Women's sport cannot be an experiment now, as it has brilliantly shown what it can do. Such a short list of events cannot be a help to women's sport propaganda, and, on the other hand, we have to think of the moral question to be considered in connection with a world meeting including men and women together."* 3

Having set up the FSFI in response to the lack of interest shown by the male sporting governing bodies, Alice Milliat had good ground to be irritated by the 'experiment' and to believe that women's athletics would be better served by women maintaining control of their own affairs.

In addition, some supporters of women's athletics felt that participation in the Olympic Games was not a priority. The reasons were as complex as the characters involved. Vice-President of the WAAA of England and FSFI member, Sophie Elliot Lynn, commented that men and women meetings were avoided in many countries because "parents were adversely disposed to them" 4 - for her, the "moral question" seemed to be the maintainance of separatism for conservative reasons.

The all-male Olympic Committee for women's sports had achieved very little for women. They agreed to five events only and Alice Milliat's FSFI had little choice. They had forced the recognition of women's sports - why should they settle for half acceptance? If they wanted to be in the Olympics the limited programme of events was the best they could get - but as if to show their scepticism they continued with their own World Games.

Great Britain's female athletes boycotted the Olympics in Amsterdam. The savage pruning of the proposed athletics programme was quite the reverse of the expansion they had hoped for, and, as they saw it, women's admission on this occasion was no more than a temporary and grudging acceptance on the part of the IOC and the IAAF.

Till minne av II. Internationella Kvinnliga Idrottsspelen från Organisationskommittén

The President and Committee of 4th Women's World Games request the honour of the company of Miss Maud Sundberg at a Banquet to be held at The Wharncliffe Rooms, Marylebone, On Saturday, August 11th, 1934, at 7.30 p.m.

R.S.V.P. to
Entertainment Hon. Sec.:
Mrs. C. Palmer,
52, Vancouver Road,
Edgware.

Hon. Sec.:
Mrs. M. Cornell,
93, Langdale Avenue,
Mitcham.

**PLEASE BRING THIS CARD WITH YOU.**

Maud Sundberg's (Sweden) mementoes from the 1926
and 1934 Women's World Games (MN)

Vera Searle Palmer said:

> "The IAAF at that time was all male. The women had their own international organisation - and the IAAF were determined that it should come to an end and they were very brutal about it. You take 1928, when the international federation decided they would have women's events in the Olympic Games. They didn't ask the women what events they wanted and what they thought was suitable. 800

*metres was deemed too strenuous; and they discarded the shot as being totally wrong for the feminine physique. And so the British women didn't go."*

Despite having many great athletes, the British women made their stand and showed their disapproval. It cannot have been a happy time for British women athletes who were in their prime and may have missed out on Olympic medals but, at that time, the athletic cause was deemed more important than the individual.

### Sophie Peirce Evans (later known as Eliott Lynn and Lady Heath)

Sophie Eliott Lynn was "a veritable amazon, standing almost six feet, weighing eleven stones, and well proportioned with it."[5] Born Sophie Peirce Evans in Knockaderry, County Limerick, on November 17th 1896, she was an all round sportswoman - tennis player, golfer, horsewoman, athlete and

*Sophie Eliott, with her silverware (SE)*

a pioneering aviator. Her athletics career spanned 1922-26 and she competed in two World Games for Britain. Sophie set Irish records in six different athletics events but her greatest achievement was in setting a world record for the Greek two arm javelin (now no longer a recognised event). At this time throwing events were with alternate hands and the best throws added together - it was thought that this made for equal development of the muscles of the arms and body and Sophie was the best in the world at that time.

Sophie holds an important place alongside Alice Milliat in pushing forward the inclusion of women in the Olympic Games and was an extraordinary character. She was instrumental in starting the English Women's Amateur Athletic Association and was elected chair in 1922.

At the IOC Congress in Prague on May 30th 1925 she was invited to speak on the question of whether or not all games were beneficial to women. She prepared two papers for the Congress: one was entitled 'Women's Participation in Athletics' and the other 'The Views of the English Women's Games Associations on the Question of Violent Games for Women.'

Her views were so sound and clearly stated that she was encouraged to write them in a book by numerous athletes and trainers (especially Mr Sam Mussabini whose work became famous to present day audiences in the film 'Chariots of Fire'). Sophie's book 'Athletics for Women and Girls' was the first of its kind to be published anywhere in Europe and the preface to it was broadcast from the BBC by Sophie on April 9th 1925.

Sophie was also an aviator who gave exhibition flights and became a professional stunt pilot. The two careers overlapped when Sophie attended the 1928 Amsterdam Olympics as a judge. She mislaid her ticket one day and was refused admittance by an over-zealous official, even though she had her judge's badge. Not a lady to be argued with, she returned to her plane and flew over the stadium threatening to land in the middle of the arena if she was not let in. Not surprisingly, the officials relented and she was admitted to get on with her judging duties.

As a pioneering aviator she set several records. Sophie made the first solo flight from Cape Town South Africa to London. One of her more unusual exploits was to see how many aerodromes it was possible to visit in a day. She called at fifty, landed in seventeen fields and refuelled six times!

Sophie was a pioneering yet complex woman. She was viewed as mentally unstable after she crashed her plane whilst flying in the United States and suffered severe head injuries. Sophie also developed an addiction to alcohol. There were rumours of her being unhappily married and about her sexuality. The impact of the violent loss of her mother, who was murdered when Sophie was a child, must have left a scar. Perhaps Sophie experienced some painful inner turmoil - but whatever happened in her private life, Sophie's place in women's sporting history is without question. At a time when women's athletics needed a voice, Sophie spoke clearly and competently. Her achievements were exceptional. Sadly, she died in 1939 after she had fallen at the bottom of a stair well of a London tram and hit her head. She was destitute and aged only forty-two.

Sophie maintained a wicked sense of humour at the end. In her will, she arranged for her ashes to be scattered from her aeroplane at midday - the exact time a certain Captain Curling, whom she thoroughly disliked, took his daily walk. Legend says that Captain Curling was smothered by Sophie's ashes and, years later, could still be heard to mutter:
"There's that Peirce lady at it again. Will I ever be clear of her?" 6

**Eliott Lynn's Advice:** (*From her book: 'Athletics for Women and Girls'*)

*"Corsets should be omitted in general life. If you feel your back wants some support, do some exercise that will strengthen the natural body wall of muscles, and do not utterly destroy it by adding an external and quite foreign body wall of string and whalebone."*

*"She should not wear stockings, for stockings have to be kept up, either by garters, which impede the circulation or suspenders, which pull against the muscles."*

*"Every game that is played in the fresh air is good, but some are better than others... Dancing is good training. The only thing coaches object to is that so often late hours and bad atmospheres are attendant upon dancing ... the quick graceful movements one sees upon the ballroom floor would be equally graceful and very efficient if translated to the track."*

*"I have played most games from school hockey up to strenuous chase of foxes at home and bigger things on the Equator, and I find that my hour or half-hour athletics twice a week is less of effort, less exhausting than any other game."*

*"Races above 1000 metres are barred for all women in this country. Too much of running tends to solidify certain ligaments and parts that are meant for easy elasticity in childbirth."*

*" It is advisable to make sure that neither the knickers nor the tunic chafe the body with any severity."*

The 1928 Olympic Games opened the door for women but, as we shall discover in the next chapter, athletics as an Olympic sport for women was still only partially acceptable. In spite of the overwhelming talent and successes of the female athletes, the IOC was still reluctant to build on the number of events, and women's athletics in the '32 and '36 Olympics was very nearly vetoed. It was hard to overcome the attitude that athletics was harmful to women and that female athletes were mannish. Alice Milliatt and the FSFI continued with the re-christened Women's World Games until 1934, and threatened to hold once again their own Olympic Games, embracing all sports, if no more events for women were added to the official Olympic programme.

Alice Milliat was clearly disheartened by the lack of progress. She wrote to the IOC in February 1935 requesting that they exclude all participation of women in the Olympic Games to allow the FSFI to organise their own games.

This radical move seem designed to help the FSFI re-establish control over women's sport, but it was too late - the FSFI were victims of their own success. They had proved that women's athletics were, in Alice's words, "brilliant" and the IAAF could now see advantages in taking control of women's affairs. The FSFI did not formally dissolve but never met again. In a letter to Alice Milliat thanking her for her work, the IAAF agreed to ratify the world records set up under the FSFI and promised that it would do its best to enlarge the programme for women in the Olympic Games.

However, in 1936, there were still only six athletics events for women in the Olympics, despite the fact that women continued competing in all kinds of running, throwing and jumping events *outside* the Games.

### Domnitsa Lanitis, Greece, Hurdler, 1936 Olympics.

"I was born in Cyprus in 1914. My father was a great lover of sports and supported the women's sports. He was the founder of the first sports club in Cyprus, 'Olympia', and he was the one who as President of this club proclaimed the women's games for participants from all the island. It was then in 1928 as a school girl that I made the first official Greek records in broad jump and high jump.

With a father who was a lover of sports and having of course a kind of talent it was only natural for me to be an athlete. I discovered I was quick in running by competing with boys in the streets. In 1931 I came to Athens with my younger sister to study at the American College. We stayed as boarders for four years. Fortunately the spirit of the school helped my athletic ambitions. I trained myself alone in the school doing all sports - basketball, volleyball, handball and track and field. I was taking part in all the Panhellenic games and every time I participated I broke records.

In 1935 the Greek Athletic Federation thought I might be a participant in the Olympic Games of 1936 and it was then in 1935 that they sent me three hurdles to the school to help my training! It was only a few months before the Olympics that I had the great privilege of a coach - of course not my own, but with all the others in all kinds of events!

In Greek society there was generally no feeling against women in sports but the Greek family was a little conservative at the time and they were not ready to see their daughters run in shorts in the stadiums. The schools also kept to the classic gymnastics or group games like volley ball. But the press was very much in favour and helpful, perhaps because it was not a usual thing and people were interested to read about it. I have papers of the time with big pictures of me and articles."

War broke out in 1939 and there were no more Olympics until 1948 in London when three more events for women - long jump, shot and 200 metres were added.

After the enormous contribution that women had made to the war effort (a contribution that had included hard manual work traditionally done by men) it was difficult for the organisers to argue that women were not strong enough to take part in athletics. But argue they did and it is only recently that a fuller competitive athletics programme for women has appeared. In the Sydney Games of 2000 twenty two athletics events for women can be seen on the programme - *seventeen* more than in 1928 when athletics for women first appeared at the Olympics.

Women now throw the hammer, triple jump and pole vault at the Olympics but in our enthusiasm to embrace these events in the Olympic programme it is worth remembering that the first world pole vault record for women was set by an American, Ruth Spencer - in 1911! Vera Searle Palmer was an early triple jumper in 1923 and Japan's Kinue Hitomi held the world best mark in 1926 with a triple jump of thirty eight feet and one and a half inches (11.62m).

So what must it have been like for those early athletes and sportswomen who forged a trail at the pre-war Olympics? A few of those who took part in the Games of 1928 (Amsterdam), 1932 (Los Angeles) and 1936 (Berlin) are still alive today to tell the tale - and though their hopes, triumphs and disappointments will strike a chord in any Olympian the world in which they competed was a very different one from that of athletes today.

# CHAPTER SIX - Amsterdam 1928

After the devastation of war on both sides of the Atlantic, the 1920s ushered in a period of hope for the future. It was a time to examine what men and women had in common, rather than what divided them. Some women were now enfranchised and the argument that women were not fit to hold public office was no longer tenable. Others felt less intimidated and less inadequate, setting themselves future goals to help realise their full equality. With their new found power and influence women wanted new experiences and began to challenge accepted traditions and question social values. They even bobbed their hair!

There was an air of optimism and self-esteem amongst women and, after the horrors of the First World War, a growing commitment to pacifism and the peace movement. Thus it seemed entirely appropriate that the release of pigeons* during the opening ceremony of the Olympics (first seen at the Amsterdam Games of 1928) should represent a new international spirit of peace. Yet the arguments and conflict about women's participation in the Olympic Games were still raging.

The first Olympic Games after World War One were held in 1920 in Antwerp. Twenty five nations competed, many of whom were still suffering from the aftermath of the conflict. The Games had stayed in Europe for 1924, when they were held in Paris and as the world prepared for the Ninth** modern Olympics in 1928, it was another European nation that was to play host.

## Amsterdam 1928

It was fourth time lucky for the Dutch - they had applied to host the Olympic Games on three previous occasions, but had not been successful. Dutch swimmer Marie Vierdag, who competed in three Olympic Games, remembers with delight the joy of competing on home territory.

> *"Amsterdam was much more of a pleasure. We had a lot of fun together. In 1928 there was no Olympic village - schools, hotels were used. I lived in my own home."*

*FOOTNOTE "The release of pigeons is a survival of the old custom at the original Olympic Games, when the pigeons were brought from the different states who were participating and actually flew home to announce the Olympic Games had opened." 1928 British Olympic Association Report.

**FOOTNOTE Although only seven had been actually held before this point, the Amsterdam Games are described as the Ninth because the Sixth Games (1916) had been cancelled due to the First World War.

Organising the Olympics was a huge undertaking and bringing together athletes from all over the world was no mean feat. In these days of supersonic aircraft, it is easy to forget the travel time it took for some nations to reach the Games - journeys over the ocean by ship that took weeks. For those crossing great distances, like the Australians, it would have an affect on their training and fitness.

When travel was time-consuming and costly, National Olympic Committees often saved money by leaving women at home but some went to the early games. For young women who had never travelled far in their own country, let alone travelled abroad, the experience of journeying to another continent was extraordinary. Alexandrine Gibb (Manager of the Canadian Women's Team in 1928) wrote that their six woman team known as the 'Matchless Six' went by ship from Quebec:

*"These girls were like any other Canadian girl athlete - full of life and fun - and anxious to enjoy the trip and pleasures it offered them. But they obediently went to bed, took care to eat wholesome foods and tried to help one another. They had one thought in mind, and that was paramount to all the other pleasures that came with the trip to Amsterdam."*[1]

*"The Matchless Six" 1928 Canadian women's track and field team. Front from left: Ethel Smith, Myrtle Cook, Jean Thompson. Middle row: Fanny Rosenfeld, Ethel Catherwood, Jane Bell. Back row: Marie Parkes (chaperone), Robert Kerr (Canadian team captain), Alexandrine Gibb (women's team captain) (NAC)*

The Australian team consisted of just four women - and the journey took an arduous six weeks. As a result the Australians had a harder time than the Canadians with their diet and athlete Edith Robinson, who was later to compete in the 100 and 800 metres, put on a stone in weight!

*Edith Robinson and the Australian team travelling over (STL)*

*"Although the trip was enjoyable we lacked the attention suitable for someone on their way to compete against the world. We played the usual deck games but it wasn't suitable for athletes, so of course we put on weight! When I arrived in*

*Edith on her marks (STL)*

*England the only time I saw a track to train on was Battersea Park, and only for a couple of days."*

There was unease about the women and men's teams travelling together, and Australian team manager Les Duff lectured the male athletes about the dangers of becoming too familiar with the women. He even had concerns about the team masseur, Roy Horton, as Edith says:

*"On the way over I wasn't allowed to have my muscles seen to. 'No man was going to massage my girls', said our manager."*

The combination of confined space, sea air and no training facilities all made things hard for the Australians. Swimmer Philomena (Bonnie) Mealing was the baby in the team and she remembers the canvas pool in which they could only take a maximum of two strokes:

*"A heavy canvas was placed over the cargo hold for our training. When the ship rolled, so did we!"*

This set-up for the Australian swimmers was hardly conducive to great swimming performances - but it was the best that could be done at the time.

*Betty Robinson, USA (USOC)*

The team from the United States made the journey across the Atlantic, and the Dutch organisers had to find all kinds of accommodation for their athletes. Betty Robinson was just 16 when she competed for the USA, and has fond recollections of her stay:

*"We lived on a boat in Amsterdam. My favourite Olympic memories are of the boat trips. I always wish I could get back on one when I see a boat on TV."*

German athlete Leni Junker competed in the 100 metres, and won a bronze in the 4 by 100 relay:

*"In Germany in 1928 there were two national sports organisations. I was a member of the Gymnastics Association and travelled alone by train third class to the Amsterdam Olympics.*

*The other three members of the relay team travelled second class as they belonged to the Sports Governing Body. You can't imagine such a thing today."*

The Australians seemed to have a difficult time even when they got to Holland, as Edith remembers:

*"There was no way of training. We were stationed 35 miles out of Amsterdam and had a bus with a chap who had never been there, so we got lost every day! It was bedlam trying to train then as we had so little time. Twice we arrived home to find the staff couldn't wait so we had to get our own meals."*

*Leni Junker, Germany (HW)*

## Opening Ceremony of the 1928 Olympic Games

At 2.00pm in the stadium on Saturday, July 28th three thousand and fourteen competitors and officials from forty six nations assembled for the official opening ceremony of the IXth Olympic Games. Headed by Greece, all the teams completed a circuit of the track, saluted the Prince Consort, Prince Hendrick, and lined up facing the Royal Box. It was a fine day and the march past lasted nearly an hour, with thirty five thousand people looking on. After a speech by Dr. J. Visser, honorary member of the Dutch Olympic Committee, an old Dutch cantata was sung by a chorus of 1,200 singers.

Amidst trumpets and cannon fire, the Olympic Flag was hoisted and the pigeons, symbolising peace, were released. Each pigeon had a ribbon bearing the colour of a competing nation tied to its neck. The Olympic Oath was taken by the captain of the Dutch football team while the Standard Bearer from each nation dipped the national flag. The athletes marched out of the stadium and the opening ceremony was over - ready for the games to begin.

## The Athletics Track and Stadium

Dutch architect Jan Wils had newly designed a grand stadium where athletics, cycling, gymnastics and equestrian events could all be held. Covering an area of about forty acres in the southern part of central Amsterdam it accommodated forty thousand spectators. In the centre of the ground was a football pitch, and surrounding it a 400 metres cinder track nearly nine yards wide in the finishing stretch. Around the running track was a cycling track 500 metres in circumference. The athletics track was still being completed forty eight hours before the opening, so practice had to be carried out in very primitive conditions on a training ground within six or seven hundred yards of the stadium. The new track had never been used before so it was extremely hard, but the quality of the surface was to produce some exceptional performances.

Opposite the Royal Box was the Marathon Gate, through which the marathon runners entered. The Marathon Tower, 150 feet high, held the plate from which a column of smoke billowed throughout the Games - the first instance of the Olympic Flame in a modern Olympics. National flags adorned the Stadium and billowed in the breeze as the women athletes took their place in the Olympic Stadium for the very first time.

## The First Olympic Athletic Event for Women - the 100 metres

It was the first time that women athletes had been admitted to the Games, so the atmosphere in the stadium was electric as the competitors lined up for the first heat of the 100 metres on Monday July 30th, at 2.15 pm.

Betty Robinson came to the Olympics with a blisteringly fast world record time of 12.0, which she ran in Chicago in June, 1928.

> *"There was not much women's track in the USA at all back in 1928. My biology teacher saw me running to catch the school train and was surprised to see me make it. He asked if he could time me at school over 50 yards and the next step was training with the boys at a club track in Chicago. There were no facilities for women but not much adverse feeling to women getting into normal sporting things like running back in the US. There were only three meets in total before I went off to the Olympics in Amsterdam."*

There were nine heats and three semi-finals before the final. Italy's Matilde Moraschi went out in the first round. Seventy years after the race, Matilde remembers her sense of injustice!

> *"There was a false start. The starter came over to me and pointed at me with his index finger, saying "YOU, YOU, YOU" - blaming me for starting first. But I wasn't, it was Bell from Canada and this was confirmed by a photograph. On the second start, I left last and last I arrived."*

Matilde will be ninety in 2000, but the accusation still rankles. She also had to contend with an amorous Frenchman, and the fear engendered in Matilde gives insight into the moral codes of the time:

*"The men's 1500m was being run and leading by a few metres was a Frenchman. Another French athlete, who was at rest like myself, came and sat beside me, all happy and full of enthusiasm. Turning towards me he said "Si Ladoumegue gagne, je vous embrasse sur la bouch" (If Ladoumegue wins, I will kiss you on the mouth). This filled me with total fear, because, at those times it would have been seen as an immoral thing, and I would have been sent home immediately. Luckily on the final lap someone else won, and all ended with disappointment for the Frenchman beside me."*

Ladoumegue got silver just behind Finland's H.E. Larva

The second semi-final of the women's 100 metres had four athletes in the race who contributed to this book - Betty Robinson (USA), who won in 12.8, Edie Robinson (Australia), Maud Sundberg (Sweden) and Leni Junker (Germany). Edie, Maud and Leni didn't make the final, but as athletes from opposite sides of the world they shared similar problems with their kit. The old concerns about women preserving their modesty and not showing too much of their bodies were still present - but they all found creative solutions!

*Maud Sundberg (Sweden) demonstrating hurdling technique to Swedish champions (MN)*

**Leni:** *"We had to bring with us our own shoes and stockings and a shovel to dig foot holes for the start. We secretly cut our shorts which we thought were too long."*

**Edie:** *"My uniform was white top and black bloomers to the knee and long black stockings. I cut the bottom of my bloomers on the ship over to Amsterdam."*

Dutch **800** metres athlete Mien Duchataeu said about the Dutch kit:

*"We wore orange woollen shorts that we knitted ourselves....Old gents said how outrageous it was - a woman in shorts!"*

Edie wanted to be able to move in her restrictive athletics clothing and Mien was fully aware of the shock she was causing by her dress - but it is worth bearing in mind that women running in shorts is still unacceptable in many cultures today.

Maud Sundberg's recollections of Amsterdam are a little different. It seems she had her mind on other things!

*"I'm a bit ashamed to tell you that my greatest memory from Amsterdam was that the men from the Mexican team followed the blue eyed girls from Sweden everywhere, and threw roses over them!"*

*Mien Duchateau, 800 metres 1928 (Holland) in uniform and in her kit (BVD)*

The final of the 100 metres held the next day was to be controversial. The day did not start too well for Betty:

*"Moments before the Olympic final I had to run back to the bus for the right shoes as I had forgotten them!"*

There were six competitors in this first ever women's Olympic track final and the tension was high. The Canadian Olympic Committee report describes the event in great detail:

*"Of the six (finalists) Miss Cook, Canadian champion, Miss Rosenfeld, of Canada, and Miss Schmidt of Germany were expected to fight it out for first place with Miss Robinson as the outside threat. Miss Cook was favored because of her record; Miss Rosenfeld and Miss Schmidt because of impressive performances in the preliminary stages.*

*Unfortunately the race was marred by the disqualification of Miss Cook and Miss Schmidt when they made two false starts. When the girls were asked to take their marks and set, Miss Cook, who is of the highly strung type, made a false break. On the second effort to get the field away she repeated her offence, Miss Schmidt offending with her. Miss Cook was eliminated. On the third effort to send the field away Miss Schmidt erred again and she also was waved to the side."* 2

Two false starts (as Matilde knew) meant that the offending competitors were disqualified. Some reports said that Canadian Myrtle Cook broke down in tears after her disqualification and that the German, Leni Schmidt, shook her fist at the starter! When the race finally got away, Betty Robinson had the best start but a tussle developed between Betty and Bobby Rosenfeld with "...the pair reaching the tape together for the closest finish of the week, a finish which left the spectators in doubt and caused the officials to go into a 'huddle' in an effort to agree upon the placing of the first two." 3

The German official who was deciding upon first place gave the decision to Betty, but the French judge spotting second place gave Betty as second - meaning that he thought Bobby had won. The chief judge (an American) gave first to Betty which was disputed by another judge (an Englishman). A representative of the Women's Federation said that Betty had won by breaking the tape with her arms and not her body as the rules said she should, so she thought Bobby should have the decision.

Ex-Olympic athlete Bobby Kerr coached the Canadian women's team and for this final had been asked to judge fifth place - which he had not had to do as only four athletes were left in. He was privy to the discussions about the final and decided to let the Canadian officials know about the dispute, especially as both the English judge and the official from the Women's Federation felt that the dispute was one for the jury to consider. Canadian team manager Alexandrine Gibb wrote out a protest about the result and took it to the officials. The protest was considered by the jury, but was disallowed. The decision led to some resentment, which the Canadian report of the games clearly voices:

> *"It has been said, many times, since the games that the rules were repeatedly violated by 'favored' nations and the records of the games, photographic and otherwise, show that the Germans and the Americans were apparently able to break the rules while other nations were invariably penalized even when they unintentionally and inadvertently violated."* 4

The Canadians were prepared to accept the rules, but were "...resentful of a spirit of favoritism which prevailed throughout the games. All they asked was a square deal for everybody." 5

Despite all the controversy, Betty Robinson was given the gold medal and set an Olympic record of 12.2 seconds. Medal ceremonies on a podium were not yet part of the Olympic scenario but the medal remained hugely important for Betty:

> *"My first Gold medal meant the most to me."*

*Finish of 1928 100 metres final from left: F. Rosenfeld (Canada) 2nd, E. Robinson (USA) 1st, E. Steinberg (Germany) 4th, E. Smith (Canada) 3rd (ANL)*

This first track medal for women - sent by post to 'little' Betty Robinson after the Olympics - marked a major event in women's athletic history, but it became insignificant in comparison with the effect the 800 metres was to have on women's athletics.

## The 800 Metres

On Wednesday August 1st there were three heats of the 800 metres. Twenty seven female competitors were entered. The first three in each heat were to go into the final the next day. In all three preliminary rounds the world record was beaten. In the final, Lina Radke of Germany lowered the record to 2 mins

16.8, and the first three finishers all bettered the world record set in the previous rounds. In 1928 these results were incredible - yet this event and any distances exceeding it were banned for women in the Games until 1960 as a result of this one race in Amsterdam. What happened?

British Olympic correspondent Sir Percival Philips submitted his report to the London Daily Mail which appeared on Friday August 3rd. The headline read **"Women Athletes Collapse - Fierce Strain of Olympic Race - Sobbing Girls"**. Sir Percival wrote that many women came to watch the race and that:

> *For them, as for everyone else, the most sensational event of the day was another exhibition of sheer exhaustion by their sisters in the arena. Nine of them took part in the final of the 800 metres flat race (roughly half a mile) and it was not a pleasant sight.*

The report was accompanied by five head shots of runners (see below) with a caption that read, "The way in which the strain of the contests tells upon women athletes at the Olympic Games may be judged from the expressions on the faces of these five women Olympic runners."

*The photo used in the Daily Mail (ANL)*

Taking a closer look at the faces featured in the newspaper, we noticed that they were, in fact, photographs taken of early rounds of the 100 metres,

*Finish of 8th heat of 100 metres. Spot the similarity? (BOA)*

yet were being used to discredit the athletes in the 800 metres! The reporting gives a clear message - women runners look ugly and will damage themselves by running. Even in those days, the media were economical with the truth.

The New York Times of August 3rd said:

> *"...this distance makes too great a call on feminine strength. At the finish 6 out of the 9 runners were completely exhausted and fell head long on the ground. Several had to be carried off the track."*

This was also untrue. The archive film footage shows one athlete falling, Canada's ace 800 metres runner, Jean Thompson, and there was a reason for her 'collapse'.

The Canadian report of the Games gives an insight into the spirit of women's athletics and the 800 metres tale unfolds in the words of Canadian Women's Team manager Alex Gibb. Of the 800 metres she says, "There is not another case of sportsmanship in the annals of Canadian athletics to equal it." 6 Her writings tell of 'little' Jeannie Thompson and 'veteran' athlete Fanny 'Bobby' Rosenfeld:

> *"Miss Rosenfeld who, all through the training period and in the sprint competitions had displayed a marvelous competitive spirit was then sent into the 800 metres race. She had never trained, in fact had never paid any attention to races at this distance, having confined herself to the sprints and the field events."* 7

Bobby, disputed silver medallist in the 100 metres, came to compete primarily in the discus! Canada's best 800 metres runner was the youngest member of the team, Jean Thompson, who was considered to be a gold medal hope until she got injured during the week leading up to the games. In the final of the 800, Jean was jostled by Japan's Kinue Hitomi. Bobby Rosenfeld:

> *".....saw it instantly and giving all she had came up from away back to get on even terms with Jeannie Thompson and talk her into finishing when she was apparently all through. And finish the youngster did with Miss Rosenfeld slowing down at the tape to let the Canadian youngster of the team finish before her. Any girl who will give up her place at the finishing line so that another girl, a teammate, can finish before her, deserves all the praise that Canadians can sing for years."* 8

It is the injured Jean Thompson who can be seen in film of the race falling at the finish, having given her all, and no-one else. Bobby Rosenfeld's selfless act and the spirit of her gesture was not mentioned in newspapers, nor the fact that some of the 'sobbing, exhausted' runners soon recovered to take part in the relay. The news reports implied that the women in the race, fine athletes like Radke and the extraordinarily talented Japanese all-rounder Kinue Hitomi, were endangering themselves by running. Great Britain's Harold Abrahams, 1924 100 metres gold medalist who found fame later in the film 'Chariots of Fire', bravely championed the athletes stating that newspaper reports of collapse were "sensational... grossly exaggerated" and that:

*"It is perfectly true to say that two or three of the competitors (one of whom I know had never run the distance before) showed signs of mild discomfort, but I incline to the view that this was more psychological than physical, and entirely to be accounted for by the natural disappointment of being beaten."*[9]

Dutch athlete Mien Duchateau competed in the third heat. She did not make the final, but had strong views retrospectively about the race:

*"Athletics was in its infancy with slow growth at this time. My training was haphazard. I trained at the local cinder track, the first in the country, with some athletes already selected for the Olympics. I had lots of stamina and competed in many events leading up to the games, my results were good and as a result of this I was included in the team myself. There was no special nutrition or specific training methods. The fact is the women's 800 metres was deleted from the programme after 1928 because of a lack of proper training."*

*Start of the women's 1928 800 metres final (ANL)*

In modern athletics, most competitors train for specific events. During the early part of the twentieth century, women who went to the Olympics often took part in a variety of events. The amazing Kinue Hitomi, who sadly died in 1931 of tuberculosis at only 24, ranks in the top hundred performers (pre-World War Two) in 100, 200 ,400, 800 metres, long jump and javelin.

It would be very surprising for a top woman athlete to excel at the highest level in sprints, middle distance running and throwing, today. Such all-round ability is best seen now in the heptathlon (seven events) and there were some pentathlons (five events) during early women's athletics meetings. In 1928, Olympic teams had few women and athletes who had gone to the Games in one event were sometimes asked to give

73

other events a try. This happened to Bobby Rosenfeld and Australian 100 metres runner, Edith Robinson, whose favourite event, the 200 metres, was not included in the programme:

> *"Even though 200 metres was too far for women to run in the Olympics, they entered me in the 800! I got talked into competing but after 600 metres I got a cramp after being in third position and I had to pull out."*

Edith did not run in the final. It would be unheard of today for an athlete to be asked to run an additional event on arrival at the Olympics - especially one that makes such different physical demands. Mien Duchateau put it succinctly:

> *"More specific adapted training methods would have prevented all the fuss."*

Lina Radke, looking over her shoulder and slowing down in the 800 metres final, can be seen on the original film footage beating Hitomi by about five yards and comfortably breaking her own world record by seven seconds. The three athletes who all broke the world record in that final never had the opportunity to run it again in the Olympics and distance running for women in the Games disappeared for the next 32 years.

The loss of Olympic competition for athletes like Lina Radke had immense consequences. Three generations of women's top middle distance runners never got to run at the Olympic Games, even though they competed in

*Edith Robinson (no. 604) in her 800 metres heat, behind Hitomi and Radke (BOA)*

athletics events and set new world figures outside the Olympics. It was a tragedy for women and the Olympic movement that the banning of distance running for women arose from sensationalist press reporting that was inaccurate and biased - reporting that is totally contradicted by the hard evidence of those who were there and the undeniable accuracy of film footage.

Alex Gibb did not pull her punches over the consequences of the 800 metres. Writing about the decision to ban the event she said:

> *"Here in Canada the feeling is that the women in charge of women's athletics should be the ones to decide these things and not the men*

*who make up the Federation (International Amateur Athletic Federation), or rather the few individuals who constitute the Federation executive, because it must be thoroughly understood that the delegates to the Federation meetings have little to say or do, everything being nicely arranged beforehand by the executive."*10

## High Jump, Discus and Relay

The high jump, discus and relay events contested for the first time in Amsterdam were not so controversial. Ethel Catherwood (Canada) became the darling of the athletics with her good looks, and Poland won its very first gold in the discus

with Halinaa Konopacka throwing an Olympic and World record of 39.62 metres (129 feet 11.8 inches.).

Bobby Rosenfeld and 'highly strung' Myrtle Cook, together with Ethel Smith and Jane Bell, were unstoppable in the 4 by 100 metres relay and set a World and Olympic record of 48.4 secs. The indomitable Bobby Rosenfeld got her well deserved gold, with Myrtle Cook running the final leg against Betty Robinson. The USA team

*Leni Junker receives the baton on the final leg of the relay (HW)*

took the silver and Germany the bronze. Leni Junker remembers her bronze with a touch of sadness:

> *"There was no Olympic presentation ceremony. My Olympic medal was sent through the post!"*

The British team, who were considered the best women's team in the world in 1928, had boycotted the Games in protest at the small number of events. This was lamented by many of the athletes who simply wanted to compete against the best. Even so, the Amsterdam Olympic Games witnessed the setting of World Records in all five athletics events - a tribute to the pioneers who were there.

*1928 Women's relay finish, Canada 1st, USA 2nd, Germany 3rd*
*Betty Robinson 2nd left, Leni Junker far left (ANL)*

## Swimming

The Olympic open air swimming pool, like the stadium, was built specially for the Olympic Games but immediately the Games finished it was to be dismantled. The 50 x 18 metres pool was adorned with flags throughout the Games and had a diving area five metres deep at one end. At the other end were the dressing areas and rooms for the swimming jury, the typists and press. Seating on three sides allowed for six thousand spectators. The water was heated up to nineteen degrees Celsius - an innovation in those days when cold water was the norm! On Saturday August 4th the swimming programme began and one of the all time greats of swimming took part - the USA's film star 'Tarzan', Johnny Weismuller. His charms were not lost on Scotland and Great Britain's young 400 metres swimmer, Sarah 'Cissie' Stewart, as she laughingly told us:

*Cissie Stewart in Olympic uniform 1928 (SH)*

*"My boyfriend! No, I wish..... but he was very handsome."*

Money was always scarce and it was not possible for everyone in 1928 to enjoy the full Olympic experience. The British women swimmers had crossed over from Harwich to the Hook of Holland on July 31st 1928, so they had missed the opening ceremony, as Joyce Cooper remembers:

*"I've never been to an opening ceremony and I've never been to a closing ceremony. The (Swimming) Association couldn't afford it. We hadn't got the money to pay for it. The boxers and swimmers never got there before the opening ceremony and had to leave before the finish."*

*Jean McDowell, left, Cissie Stewart, centre and Ellen King, Scottish champions off to Amsterdam (JB)*

Cissie Stewart:

*"We were provided with a Panama hat with the band in Association colours, a blazer with the Union Jack on the pocket, a white dress, a tie in association colours and a swim suit and bath robe. We provided our own brown shoes and flesh coloured stockings. The uniform had to be worn at all functions. The Games had already started when we arrived in Amsterdam so we missed the opening ceremony, but coming to the pool and seeing all those flags right round, to me that was a really tremendous feeling. I had never seen anything like that before."*

*1928 British team in Holland, Joyce Cooper back row far right, Jean McDowell middle row left, Cissie Stewart front row left (IG)*

Cissie was one of the first in action on the first swimming day in the 400 metres freestyle and drawn against the great American swimmer, Martha Norelius, gold medallist in Paris 1924. Martha had set seventeen world records before coming to the Games and another world record in Cissie's heat.

Cissie, suffering from a minor operation on her arm, came in second. In the semi-final, against Norelius again, she set a personal best to qualify for the final. Cissie remembers:

> "I was told to try to get through each round. It was hard going, each heat I swam in I was always up against Norelius, I thought oh! no, here we go again! But I managed to get to the final and I think they (British officials) were quite pleased with that"

In fact it was said that Cissie gave one of the 'pluckiest"[11] finishes of the whole tournament when she swam into fourth place after being last at half way and looking hopelessly out of the race. Martha won the gold, Marie Braun, daughter of the Dutch swimming coach 'Ma' Braun, silver and Josephine McKim the bronze.

Next up was the 100 metres backstroke where Great Britain's Joyce Cooper put in a very good performance winning a bronze medal.

The BOA report described this as the 'finest contest in the whole of the tournament',12 which was narrowly won by Marie Braun in 1 min. 22 seconds. The British swimmer Ellen King finished second, just a fifth of a second behind Marie, and Joyce was third, three-fifths of a second behind Ellen. Without electronic timing, hand held stop watches showed that was a very close finish.

A poetic fan of Joyce's wrote in the 'Swimming Times', after Joyce Cooper's 1928 Amsterdam performance:

> *'Joyce of the Mermaids hath neither brawn nor beef*
> *Joyce swims with courage, and grace beyond belief;*
> *Joyce, nothing loathe,*
> *In the spirit of the oath,*
> *Had a stab at back and free, and won a place in both!'*

In the 100 metres freestyle, Scottish swimmer Jean McDowell won her first heat. Jean sprang a 'surprise'13 when she swam above her form to beat the American, Laird. The two British girls, Jean and Joyce Cooper, had to race each other in the 100 metres freestyle final and both set personal bests, but a dramatic story was to unfold.

Once again the final was extremely close. The Americans, Albina Osipowich and Eleanor Garathy, drew away over the last fifty metres and touched almost together, as did Jean and Joyce. The judges decided Albina touched first with Eleanor second. The newspapers reported the difficulty in deciding who got the touch for the bronze medal. Some thought that Jean had got the touch but the judges gave it to Joyce by three votes to two. Despite the

*Start women's 100 metres freestyle, featuring Jean and Joyce's tussle for bronze (IG)*

disappointment for Jean, it never interfered with her very good friendship with Joyce which has lasted over 70 years. Jean recalled:

> *"It was very close coming to the end, but I thought Joyce touched after me. Joyce's coach was shouting 'You were third, Joyce, you were third.' Whether or not he knew she was, I don't know."*

Joyce: *"I know Jean had hard luck. Really hard luck. She and I had a lot of very good races."*

Jean had yet more disappointment to come. The swim off for the relay team places was held in Amsterdam because the weather had been so bad at the British team trials in Blackpool:

> "We had a team trial and they didn't even clear the pond for our trial. You'll not believe this, I swam and someone who was in my path sank himself down underneath me and came up on top of me while I was swimming and, of course, I swam badly and they put Cissie Stewart in my place."

Cissie: "I did Jean out of her place. It really should have been Jean. This was a big surprise to me because I really wasn't a 100 metres swimmer, I was a long distance swimmer, however at Amsterdam when the six of us swam off in the trial I came fourth and poor old Jean was knocked out"

Jean: "Cissie was usually two seconds slower than me so I thought I was very hard done by. When it came to the actual race I was two seconds faster than her. So I felt I had a bad Games, what with losing my third place and losing my place in the team. But I got over it."

Such individual dramas are the essence of the Olympic Games. Cissie gave a great performance on her leg of the relay, and with Joyce, Vera Tanner and Ellen King went on to win a silver medal, finishing second to the great American team who broke the Olympic record.

The outstanding female swimmer of 1928 was undoubtedly Martha Norelius, whilst the pool-side was dominated by the awesome Dutch coach 'Ma' Braun who was encouraging her own daughter Marie, and the other Dutch swimmers, including Marie Vierdag. Marie Vierdag went out in the semi-final of the 100 metres free, but her moment was to come at the Olympic Games in Los Angeles four years later.

*'Ma' Braun in ferocious action (IG)*

## Fencing

The Olympic fencing took place in a pavilion erected close to the stadium, which for the first time enabled fencers to feel much more part of the Games. The roof of the pavilion and upper parts of the wall at each end were made of glass shaded with curtains at the western end, which could be drawn against the evening sun - an important detail in fencing. Large scoring boards, a new feature, were easily read by the  spectators who were easily able to keep up to date with the progress in the different 'pools'. The fencing was well attended and regularly and keenly watched by the Dutch Prince Consort.

Women fencers in the Twenties were not exempted from Victorian demands to preserve their modesty and the 1928 Olympics fencing rules insisted that "bloomers of the ladies must be covered by a skirt which must be at least knee length." 14

This second appearance of women's fencing in the Games was contested by twenty eight competitors in the individual foil competition which took place on pitches laid with cork lino. Eight matches were able to take place at once, and the contestants were  divided into four pools, the first four in each pool passing into the semi-final.

The final group of eight fencers consisted of three from Germany, two from Great Britain and one each from Hungary, Belgium and Holland.

*Muriel Freeman, Great Britain 1928, silver medallist, right, with Gwendoline Nelligan, Great Britain, fencing in Lincoln's Inn Fields (MF)*

Muriel Freeman from Great Britain narrowly lost to the famous German fencer, Helene Mayer, by seven wins to six. Madame Olga Oelkers, also from Germany, came third. The brave Miss de Boer from Holland came in eighth position and received a total of 33 hits. She gave 23 hits which was only two less than the bronze position - her defence let her down!

**Eleanor Baldwin Cass, USA,** was a teacher of fencing in 1928 and like previous pioneering women wrote a book based on her experiences entitled 'The Book of Fencing'. Her friend Edwin Markham recognised her wisdom and wrote this poem to her.

### The Woman With The Foil

*I see you, woman, with the lunge and parry,*
*With grace and charm and might -*
*Coming with high heart, brave and blithe and airy,*
*Out of ancient night.*

*This is your freedom, this your day of daring*
*Your freedom from the past;*
*Come with your noble pride and prowess, weaving*
*Your womanhood at last.*

*Once you were only slave to crib and kitchen,*
*As drab as pot and pan;*
*While men were haughty, free, and only rich in*
*The brawn that makes a man*

*Or else you were a butterfly of fashion*
*The key of some dull duke,*
*The plaything of his pageant or his passion*
*Or of his rude rebuke.*

*Stand forth, O woman, free of pains and pallor -*
*Stand forth under the sky,*
*And teach men how to greatly live in valor,*
*And how to greatly die.*

*Edwin Markham, 1928*
*Inscribed to my friend Eleanor Cass*

1928 marked the first medal appearance of Helene Mayer, who was to achieve notoriety eight years later at the 1936 Berlin Olympics.

## Gymnastics

For the first time in 1928 an official gymnastics competition had been included in the Olympic programme for women, after the very successful international demonstrations at previous Games. Only five nations, Italy, Holland, Great Britain, Hungary and France contested the event. The competition was for a team of ten gymnasts on parallel bars of even height, pommel horse, a team drill of free exercises and jumping exercises. The women used exactly the same apparatus as the men in their first competition. The asymetrical bars and vaulting horse were to be introduced later.

*The 'Prim and Proper' British bronze medal team (MW)*

*The same team in a daring pose (MW)*

Clothing continued to be an issue for all sportswomen at these Games. The British gymnastics team of 1928 were heavily criticised when they posed for their team photograph revealing too much of their shapely legs. On no account were they to show their knees, even in thick black stockings! They were required to dress modestly, and wore black stockings under gym tunics when they made their competitive Olympic debut in Amsterdam. Even the team photograph showing crossed legs was frowned upon!

It was not decent to show any contours or any womanly shape (a difficult problem as many of the 1928 gymnasts were married women and not, as today, pre-pubescent girls) and so the women had to bind their breasts with wide bandages while competing. Blouses underneath their tunics and ties helped the British women to conceal their bodies even more. This probably didn't help their movement and may explain why the gymnasts at this time were not performing somersaults!

The first Gold medal for team gymnastics in 1928 was won by the Netherlands, with Italy taking silver and Great Britain bronze. Ethel Seymour of Great Britain became the oldest

*Carrie Pickles (GB) in gymnastic uniform (GL)*

gymnastic medallist winning her bronze at the age of 46 years and 6 months. A distinction unlikely to be seen today!

Unbeknown to the successful Dutch team, some of them would be fighting an even greater battle of courage and endurance and find themselves facing indescribable trials and challenges in future years. Almost half the 1928 team and one of their two coaches were Jewish or of Jewish descent. Estella Blits-Agsterribe died in Auschwitz. Fellow team members Helena Kloot-Nordheim, Anna Dresden-Polak, team reserve Judikje Themans-Simons and their highly popular coach Gerrit Kleerekoper disappeared with their partners, young

*1928 Olympic gymnastic demonstration by Dutch gymnasts (IOC)*

children and many relatives in the horror of Sobibor. *15*

The sole surviving Dutch gymnastics team member and gold medallist Alie van den Bos appeared on a Dutch television programme during 1999. Her tears as well as her words told that she has never forgotten her team mates:

> *"Terrible things happened to those Jewish girls."*

## On to Los Angeles

The Amsterdam Olympics marked an important point in women's Olympic history - athletics, albeit in a limited form, had appeared for the first time amid huge controversy. The British women who had boycotted the athletics events had some hard thinking to do in the next four years - could they accept the limited programme or would they maintain their radical stance? What position would Alice Milliat and the FSFI adopt in response to the banning of the 800 metres? Gymnastics had also made its first competitive appearance and fencing was now established as a regular Olympic sport for women. The swimming events had seen several world records tumble - minds and bodies were set for Los Angeles.

# CHAPTER 7 - Los Angeles 1932

In 1932 the Olympic Games were held for the second time in America, on this occasion in Los Angeles. In 1904 in St. Louis, the first time the Olympics were held on American soil, only six women participated and they were all American archers. In Los Angeles, a hundred and twenty seven women took part in three sports, swimming, fencing and athletics - one sport less than the Amsterdam Olympics. Women's gymnastics was not included this time in the programme. A trip to California was a long and expensive journey for many competing nations and there was a significant reduction in the number of competitors, in particular women, who were outnumbered ten to one by the men.

## Good Guys 3
### Gustav Kirby, President of the American Athletic Union

*Gustav Kirby threatened to cancel the men's programme when the IOC wanted the women's athletics removed from the programme of the 1932 Olympics.*

There had been big changes in women's lives during the Twenties, but the early Thirties saw a time of world-wide economic depression. The British women had finally made up their mind to embrace the Games, but sent a team of just five. Money was very tight. Violet Webb was a member of Great Britain's very first female Olympic athletics team:

> *"Our expenses were paid, but when I came home I was asked to pay seventeen shillings and sixpence for my Olympic tracksuit, so I didn't even get that free!"*

## Journey to LA

For those who did make the trip, like those who went to Amsterdam, it was to prove unforgettable. Dutch swimmer Marie Vierdag:

> *"In 1932 we had a wonderful trip to Los Angeles, by boat from Rotterdam to New York and by train from coast to coast. The whole trip took two months and we visited all the highlights of the beautiful country."*

The British team also travelled by ship and went from Southampton. Violet Webb's eyes shone when she recalled the journey.

*"It took five days to cross the Atlantic. Our fellow passengers were Prime Minister Stanley Baldwin and his Cabinet. They were going out to the Ottawa conference. We used all the first class facilities, they couldn't do anything else but let us use them. We used to run around the decks, do whatever we could. There was a small pool for the swimmers. It was really a fantastic trip across the Atlantic. Lord Burley, our captain, was on the boat with his wife. We spent a week on the train across country. It was only for athletes. I think the Irish and South Africans, perhaps the Canadians too, were on it, and whenever it stopped we ran up and down the station platform to keep fit and then jumped back on the train!"*

At just seventeen years old, she took the train down to Chicago - a trip that allowed her to view the beautiful Rocky Mountains. She said that she had never seen anything quite like it. Even for an American, the journey was special, as USA swimming gold medallist Helen Johns, World and Olympic record holder in the 4 by 100 metres freestyle relay, discovered:

*"The Olympic Special train from New York had seventeen cars, one air conditioned and one a gym. We were on board three nights and four days - a great way to see the United States."*

Javelin thrower Tilly Fleischer was twenty one when she travelled over with the German team:

*"We sailed from Bremenhaven to New York with the Europa, at that time the fastest ship in the world. We were met by the mayor, Jimmy Walker. A huge crowd of German-Americans welcomed us in Central Park. We travelled four days and four nights with the Santa Fé to Los Angeles. No-one would do this today - nowadays you can fly in six to eight hours."*

The competing nations arrived in Los Angeles - a city with a desire to create the best Olympiad ever, but trapped in deep economic depression.

## Winner's podium for the first time

The Los Angeles Coliseum, built in 1921 and enlarged in 1930 to hold over a hundred thousand spectators, was the main stadium. The running track had a new surface of crushed peat and, for the first time, there appeared a three-tiered victory stand for the medal presentation ceremonies. Many of the winning athletes standing on this podium to receive their medal cite this experience as their most important Olympic memory, one that has always remained with them. Violet Webb enthused:

> *"It was wonderful, wonderful. It was an awe-inspiring thing to go and compete in this fabulous stadium that you must have seen in 1984. The opening ceremony was absolutely fabulous. You felt proud, you were British, as you paraded around. The biggest thing, when you see them standing on the rostrum now, with the tears, I can understand how they feel because it was like that for us. When we stood on the rostrum, just the four of us, when the Union Jack went up it is amazing. If you are proud of your country you do feel that way."*

Helen Johns won gold, and agreed:

> *"When we won I felt I had done a small thing to bring honor to the United States. I was overcome with emotion when the USA flag went up and the Star Spangled Banner was played."*

Australian swimmer from the 1936 Olympics, Evelyn de Lacy, said:

> *"I think the greatest moment in any athlete's life is to stand on the dais and hear the National Anthem played and watch their country's flag being raised. I still believe that today."*

## Olympic Village

At each Olympics since 1924 the Organising Committees have provided an Olympic Village to house the athletes. In Los Angeles a village of 550 small houses were constructed, but still the women were barred from going there. The Organising Committee felt that feminine needs could be better met in a permanent type of residence and the Chapman Park Hotel was considered the most suitable. The Chapman was a first class hotel, close to the training grounds, in an exclusive and beautiful district, and convenient for shopping! It was so close to Hollywood that movie stars were often to be spotted at the hotel as well as the stadium and several of the women interviewed in their eightieth and ninetieth years still remember the stars they met. Violet recalled:

*Eva Dawes (second left) and Canadian team 1932 with actress Norma Shearer (ES)*

*"We used to sit with all the film stars in the stand - it was much more relaxed, in a way, than it is today. We were quite near Hollywood and we used to be entertained by the film stars. We would go there and they would take us all around. We met Snozzle Durante, Janet Gaynor, Charles Farrell.... it was just wonderful."*

Underneath the Hollywood glitz was a grimmer reality, which did not escape the eyes of the competitors. Helen Johns:

*"I clearly remember Los Angeles in 1932. The Olympic atmosphere was upbeat, the stadium wonderful, the pool large and beautiful, but it was the depression and Los Angeles was sad to see - empty stores and signs: 'Beds 10 cents a night.'"*

## Los Angeles Coliseum

Even though life was tough for many, a crowd of more than a hundred thousand paying customers flocked to the Coliseum on the morning of Saturday, July 30th 1932 to be in plenty of time for the Opening Ceremony of the Los Angeles Games later that afternoon. Another fifty thousand who couldn't get a ticket, or couldn't afford one, milled around outside. Thirty seven countries were attending and the American Vice-President, Charles Curtis, deputising for President Hoover, declared the Games open at 2.30 pm. The crowd enjoyed the spectacle of an artillery salute, a massed choir twelve hundred strong and a two hundred and fifty piece band playing the National Anthem. Many writers of the time commented on how moving the ceremony had been. Once the traditional ceremonies were over, the pigeons released and the Olympic flag raised, the spectators left their seats, eagerly anticipating what was to come in the next few days.

The Track and Field events started the following day, July 31st, and lasted until August 7th. Fifty four women athletes represented eleven countries in the six events. In each event the world record was equalled or beaten. Not one champion from 1928 returned to the 1932 Games to defend her title, so all the winners were first time Olympic champions.

After the 'debacle' of the 800 metres in Amsterdam there was to be no repeat of the event at these games and no opportunity to show how standards had improved. A number of people still disapproved of women in athletics, especially journalists and some members of the IOC. American women physical educators were opposed to training a few women for the Olympics at the expense of meeting the needs of the majority. They campaigned against sending a team to Los Angeles, but the popularity of athletics and swimming won the day and the dominance and success of the American women more than repaid the cost.

## Athletics

The first women's athletics event was held on Sunday July 31st - the javelin, a substitute event for the discredited 800 metres. Unchanging attitudes towards women competitors were noted by columnist Westbook Pegler. In the *Chicago Tribune* of August 1st 1932, he wrote that women taking part in field events had caused consternation among male sports writers. Many of these men insisted that:

> "...women's place in the Olympic meets is in the water and not on land and (so) urge that they be...prevented from cluttering up the lot with delicate parodies of the mighty feats that males perform." 1

## Good Guys 4

**Captain F.A.M. Webster, British athletics coach, author of 'Athletics of Today For Women'**

*"The disadvantages of women taking part in athletics are, I honestly believe, far more apparent than real....the benefit to be derived far outweighs any disadvantages which may have to be faced." (1930)*

*Tilly Fleischer (IOC)*

Germany's Tilly Fleischer came from a different, highly-physicalised culture and never seemed to feel that her gender was an issue. The idea that she might be a 'delicate parody' was not part of her experience, and the support of the German government in the development of the health and fitness of the nation undoubtedly helped the German women athletes of the 1930s to excel. Tilly saw both men and women athletes as deeply principled - if a little broke:

> *"Men and women were not treated differently in sports, and it wasn't unusual for women to take part in sport. We all bought our own training and sports gear ourselves. Every one an idealist. We received one dollar per day as pocket money - but only when we reached Los Angeles."*

Tilly came into the javelin event as one of the favourites, and later described the Los Angeles Games as 'low key.' She finished in bronze medal position behind the most famous athlete of '32 - Babe Didrickson - but went on to greater things in 1936 at her 'home' Games.

## Babe Didrikson

Mildred 'Babe' Didrikson remains one of the greatest women athletes of the twentieth century. She excelled at every sport she tried and was given the name 'Babe' after the great baseball player Babe Ruth, when she hit so many home runs. Babe Didrikson was also well known as a basketball player before attending the US track and field championships. In a most incredible afternoon at the US championships, Babe won five events, tied a sixth and set two world records in just three hours.

In the 1932 Olympic Games women athletes were not allowed to exert them-selves to this degree, and were restricted to competing in just three individual events. This ruling denied the world seeing what exceptional women athletes like Babe could achieve. Having won the javelin, Babe's next event was the 80 metres hurdles. For fellow American hurdler, Evelyne Hall, Babe's second gold came at her expense, for the finish was so tight that it took the judges half an hour to make their decision.

A first in Los Angeles was the use of an electrical timing device called the 'Kirby Two Eyed Camera,' but that didn't help the judges to decide on the winner. A photograph taken track side clearly showed both athletes had tied. In an interview with the Los Angeles Times, 5th August, 1932 Babe said that she had "slowed up a little...I just wanted to make it a good race". 2 Her arrogance rankled with many of Babe's rivals. Violet Webb, who had set a world record in the hurdles in 1931, competed against Babe in the hurdles and remembered Babe as very business-like, unusual for the time, not very chatty and totally focused on what she was going to do. Babe got the judges' decision, but her insensitivity to Evelyne Hall was marked and Babe had to endure a lot of criticism for her single-mindedness. Had Babe been a man, it is likely that her will to win would have been praised as an asset - but as a woman it made her very unpopular.

In her third event, the high jump, which was held later in the week, the decision went against Babe. She jumped the same height as the winner Jean Shiley, but the judges labelled Babe's style of jumping as diving - though archive footage shows Babe's style to be very much like the Western Roll.* Ruling that Babe's head had crossed before her feet, Shiley was pronounced the winner and Babe given second. Strangely, *both* were credited with a new world record jump and a question remains as to why the judges did not warn Babe about her jumping style earlier in the competition, or even disqualify her. Canadian athlete Eva Dawes was awarded bronze. When asked why Babe wasn't disqualified from the competition, she said:

> "Well, why wasn't she? I don't know why. The style then was scissors. They said she dived. When I look back now, I should have made a fuss. I just accepted it."

Babe Didrikson remains the only athlete in Olympic history to win medals in individual running, jumping and throwing events.

*Jean Shiley, Babe Didrikson and Eva Dawes (ES)*

Amid all the controversy about the 80 metres and the high jump, the discus passed by simply and cleanly. American Lilian Copeland threw 40.58 metres for gold, with fellow US teamate Ruth Osburn taking silver and Poland's Jadwiga Wajsacowna the bronze.

FOOTNOTE* A style of jumping which, along with the straddle, became common place in high jumping during later years. In the Western Roll, the jumper turns sideways and goes over the bar horizontally, looking at the ground as she jumps. In the prevailing scissors jump of the time, the legs were swung as high as possible (like scissors) and the jumper remained vertical throughout the jump and looked upwards. It is worth remembering that the jumpers were landing on sand - not the luxurious inflatables of today.

## Black Women At The Olympic Games

### First Black American women selected for Olympic Athletics Team

Tidye Pickett and Louise Stokes, Los Angeles 1932. Both were excellent sprinters but were not selected for the individual events or the relay at the Olympic Games of 1932. The USA team stopped en route to Los Angeles in Denver where a dinner was held in their honour. All the team were invited - except Tidye and Louise who were separated from the others and took dinner in their room.

### First Black Woman to win Olympic Gold Medal

Alice Coachman (USA) in London 1948, High Jump.

### First Black African woman to win Olympic Gold Medal

Deratu Tulu in Barcelona 1992 10,000 metres.

## Stella Walasiewicz and the 100 metres

In the 100 metres race, the USA were without their 1928 Olympic Champion, Betty Robinson, who had been badly injured in a plane crash. In the final, the Polish sprinter Stella Walasiewicz (later called Walsh) took gold, with Canada's Hilda Strike second and the USA's Wilhelmina (Billie) von Bremen third. Stella, who was living in America, had been expected to take American citizenship and run for the USA but at the last moment she chose to run for the country of her birth, Poland. Stella was renowned for attending track events already dressed to compete and leaving immediately afterwards, which led to speculation about her sex.

Violet Webb remembered several women on the circuit during the 1930s whom she described as 'hefty' and who were the subject of some discussion amongst the athletes. Vera Searle Palmer, by now Honorary Secretary of the English Women's AAA, said:

> "I know some women shaved in the mornings!"

Vi added that "It didn't necessarily mean that they were men" but even in the Twenties and Thirties there were suspicions that some competitors in women's sports were male. Italian sprinter of the 1930s, Fernanda Bullano, still cherishes a photograph signed to her personally by Stella Walsh. Fernanda remembers:

> "I met Stella first in London (at the Women's World Games of 1934),

*and saw her again in Berlin. She was a reserved, timid girl but we Italians understood that she was being friendly towards us and we liked her a lot."*

Stella Walsh came to a very sad end in 1980, when she was shot during an attempted robbery at a store where she was shopping. A post-mortem revealed that she did indeed have male sex organs. Issues of gender and sexuality are complex and extend far beyond the presence of male or female sex organs or chromosome counts. Whether or not the presence of some male sex organs gave Stella Walsh an advantage in her running is something that we are unlikely to ever know for sure - but her life and tragic death clearly show that difficulties in gender testing are nothing new.

## The Relay and First British Athletic Medal

*Violet Webb returning home from Los Angeles to a celebratory welcome from her work colleagues (SR, JC)*

The final of the relay was held on Sunday August 7th, the last day of the track and field events. The US coach George Vreeland was determined to win the relay after the 'failure' of the American women to win the 100 metres. He picked his team very carefully, considering the strengths of each runner, and then drilled them in the art of fast baton-changing. The Canadians, gold medalists and Olympic record-holders from Amsterdam, possessed a strong squad and were seen as the main threat.

Top British sprinter, Ethel Johnson, had strained a hamstring in the preliminary rounds of the 100 metres, so Violet Webb took her place in the 4 by 100 metres relay and ran the long second leg. The Canadians and Americans were neck-and-neck coming into the final straight, but the American Billie Von Bremen managed to see off the challenge of Canada's Hilda Strike, winning by a yard. The British team had their own struggle with the Dutch, but held their third place to pick up bronze. This performance resulted in the very first track and field medal won by British women at the Olympics Games, and was a memory held very dear by Violet.

*"We were proud that we brought back a medal, even if it was only a bronze medal in the relay."*

## Swimming

The Olympic swimming competition took place between August 6th and 13th in a stadium holding ten thousand spectators. With a similar number of entries to athletics, thirteen countries and fifty five swimmers and divers took part in the five events. It was to be a fantastic games for the USA team and a star, Helene Madison, was to be born.

The Americans had a far more professional approach to their training than other competing countries, and their women were dominant. Relay gold medalist Helen Johns:

> *"Training was hard work, nerve racking at times, but enjoyable. Facilities favored the boys but the boys were intimidated if you were good."*

A packed stadium watched Helene Madison win the 100 and 400 metre freestyle, Eleanor Holm the 100 metres backstroke and the USA team the 4 by 100 metres relay. Springboard diving went to Georgia Coleman, and high diving to Dorothy Poynton. The exception to the USA's dominance was Claire Dennis of Australia, who won the 200 metres breaststroke.

*1932 gold medal winning USA relay team, from left, Josephine McKim, Helen Johns, Eleanor Garatti-Saville and Helen Maddison (HC)*

## Disappointment For Joyce

For 1928 British Amsterdam Olympic medalist, Joyce Cooper, the games were disappointing. She was entered for four events (women swimmers were exempt from the 'three event only' rule which had prevented Babe Didrickson from competing in additional events) and the toll of swimming in heats and finals told on her. Speaking in 1998 Joyce said:

> *"My greatest sadness was in the 1932 Olympics. I was selected for everything but was told to concentrate on the 400 as we hadn't got anyone else, then I had a message from the team manager who said I was not to swim in the heats of the 400 but to save myself for the relay. I couldn't find the team manager but asked the team captain*

*and chaperone what they felt about it. They said, 'As long as you promise not to gut yourself and treat it as a training session it will be all right.' I hadn't had any time for relaxed training so I decided to do it. When the team manager heard he was furious! We came third in the relay, but when I swam in the 100 metres backstroke final against world record holder Eleanor Holm after leading I blew up and struggled home. The dear team manager said 'told you so.' I was very sad because I'd just done what I thought was right for myself and the team."*

Joyce came fourth in the 400 metres final. She was still trained by Bill Howcroft who was recognised as one of the great swimming coaches of the era. Swimming in four events meant that Joyce's disappointment was not confined to the backstroke:

*"In the 100 metres freestyle semi-final the first three went through to the final. I missed my touch and came in fourth, with a faster time than the other semi was won in. The Americans and Dutch wanted me to swim in the seventh lane but I didn't want them changing the rules for me. I was most disappointed in the 100."*

Joyce, who was quite frail as a child, still struggled with her health.

*"The troublesome pain in my abdomen was not diagnosed until the mid 1930's. It often caused me to collapse at the end of the race and go unconscious."*

*The 1932 British Olympic team, Joyce Cooper sitting 3rd from right (IG)*

It later transpired that Joyce had been swimming for some years with an ovarian cyst. She came away from the 1932 Olympics without an individual medal - but was an extremely popular competitor. She went on to swim throughout the world, and in 1934 found herself competing in Australia against a young Australian and future Olympic swimmer, Pat Norton. Joyce defeated Pat in the final of the 100 metres freestyle, and a newspaper cutting from Pat's scrap book, dated January 1st 1934, said:

## "WE DIPS THE LID TO JOYCE COOPER BUT OH! OUR PAT."

### ENGLISH MERMAID MOOTED IN THRILLING 'HUNDRED' AND JUST PIPPED BONDI LASS.

*Miss Cooper has made herself wonderfully popular since her arrival and her victory was pleasing to everyone, but perhaps the greatest tribute to her likeable nature was the presentation to her by Harry (Bull) Hellings of a floral tribute to her on behalf of the Domains Baths staff who also decorated her dressing room in grand style. 'Bull' had never done that before to anybody, and they know their swimmers. Nuff said!"*

*Joyce Cooper and Pat Norton in NSW State title 100 yards freestyle in 1934 (PD)*

*NSW Swimming Championships 1934, Pat Norton (1st right), Joyce Cooper (2nd left) (PD)*

Marie Vierdag (MS)

## Elation for Bonnie and Marie!

After her disappointment at Amsterdam, Australia's Bonnie Mealing excelled herself, winning silver in the 100 metres backstroke behind Eleanor Holm and beating Joyce, who finished fifth. From what Bonnie wrote later, it was quite an outstanding effort!

*"My greatest achievement was winning the silver at Los Angeles, and my two world records. I had no coach - didn't train over - much. I liked tennis and golf and played both occasionally. What made me take up swimming? I liked it for fun , but was never keen on competition!"*

At her third Olympics, Marie Vierdag finally won a medal - a cherished silver in the relay.

## Fencing

The third sport at the 1932 games for women was fencing and the individual foil. It was here that Helene Mayer of Germany, who was to become a controversial figure in the 1936 Berlin Olympics, was defending her 1928 Olympic title. There were several surprises.

Helene Mayer, the European Champion, was beaten by British fencer Heather Guiness, and Peggy Butler and Marion Lloyd, the British and USA champions, failed to reach the final pool.

The final was a keen one and was contested between Ms Guiness and Ms Preis (Austria). A new champion was to emerge, as a newspaper of the time reported:

*"Preis did the attacking and lunged furiously at the British girl. Ms Guiness refused to be flurried and skilfully turned aside many of her opponents ripostes. Consistent attack, however, on the part of Ellen Preis, succeeded in gaining for her the title by five hits to three"*

Heather Guiness took silver and Ena Bogen (Hungary) bronze. This was the start of Ellen Preis' illustrious Olympic career and she went on to become the first woman to compete over a twenty-four year period, 1932-1956.

## Taking Part or Winning?

> *"The most important thing in the Olympic Games is not to win but to take part, just as the most important thing in life is not the triumph but the struggle. The essential thing is not to have conquered but to have fought well."* 3

Baron de Coubertin's famous words were displayed on the score board for the first time in Los Angeles. In the light of increasing professionalism in sport these words may ring hollow for some Olympians today, but they are still held dear by many others. The women who competed in 1932 have their own view. The swimmer who captivated 'Bull' Hellings in Australia, Joyce Cooper, always 'gutted' herself to the extent that she would disappear exhausted under the water at the end of a race said:

> *"I was always wanting to beat the others, I was competitive but people were always lecturing me, 'Joyce, you have to hate your enemies', but I could never get myself to that pitch. I can honestly say that my greatest friends were the people I raced against."*

Joyce's feelings about competition are more complex. In a voice heaving with emotion she said:

> *"The thing that moved me most was not having the Union Jack go up at the Olympics on the main post. To me as a youngster your greatest pride is in your school, your sport, your country, and as you go through life whatever you do you do to the best, whatever that is. It is the most important thing, and I think during those eight years, even to this day, I would have given anything to help get the Union Jack on the top... but I didn't."*

Violet Webb echoed some of those feelings:

> *"I didn't go out to get a medal, I went out to do my best, that's all you can do. It was wonderful, all the different countries, we used to mix even if we didn't speak the same language, we managed to get on together."*

The Olympic motto 'Citius, Altius, Fortius' - 'Faster, Higher, Stronger' was encapsulated in Babe Didrickson's performances at the Los Angeles Games, and Joyce and Violet's words mirror Baron de Coubertin's dreams of bringing together the 'youth of the world' in friendly competition. Despite the depression, the 1932 Los Angeles Games were deemed a success, and many of the athletes who took part were eagerly anticipating the next Olympics four years on in Berlin. But already a shadow was rising in Germany - a shadow that was to hang over the most spectacular Olympics so far.

# CHAPTER 8 - Images of the Berlin Olympics 1936

It is ironic that it had been planned to hold the 1916 Olympic Games in Berlin when the First World War had prevented it. Now in 1936 the Games had at last reached that city, but again the storm clouds of conflict were gathering.

A serious question mark hung over the Berlin Olympics of 1936. The politics of racism that were an inherent part of Adolph Hitler's Germany led to threats of a boycott of the Games. IOC member Avery Brundage visited Germany to see if international law was being upheld and if people were being oppressed. On his return, Brundage declared that the Games should go ahead. He held the view that the IOC should not interfere with the politics of a host nation. The Germans had taken steps to include a Jewish athlete in its Summer Olympic team - Helene Mayer the fencer - but life for other Jewish athletes was less tolerable. Despite that, the decision was made to keep the Games in Germany.

The Worker's Sport Association had tried to stop the 1936 Olympic Games being held in Berlin and organised an alternative Olympics in Barcelona, which was cancelled when the Spanish Civil War had broken out. Eva Dawes who competed in 1932, had upset the Canadian Olympic Commitee and the Athletics Federation when she attended an athletics meeting in Russia and had been suspended as a consequence. Her decision to attend the Barcelona Games was equally unpopular. In 1999, Eva said:

*Alice Arden and Marjorie Gestring (USA) on board the SS Manhatten (AH)*

*"I had upset the Federation because I accepted an invitation and went without telling them and so they barred me from the 1936 Olympics. Barcelona was having a mini-Olympics and I accepted an invitation from them which upset the Federation again. They hadn't got anyone to represent Canada in the high jump for the 36 Olympics and they wrote to me and asked if I would like to be re-instated and I said no. They had already banned me and that was it."*

Today, Eva maintains that her decisions about where and when she competed were motivated by her interest in travel and not political views that many ascribed to her. What is undoubtedly clear is that she disliked anyone telling her what to do - including the Canadian Federation.

However, the athletes who attended these Olympic Games were stepping into the black shadow of World War II. Australian swimmer Pat Norton's political awareness was about to grow:

> "I was very conscious of taking part in a politically-motivated Olympiad. Though only seventeen I was very politically minded, which was cultivated by the turbulent Jack Lang* days, when I would join the crowd while the budding politician was pleading his case. The wit and heckling was great! My trip to Berlin was to develop my international politics.
>
> In Marseilles we popped into a Newsreel and watched a short on Herr Hitler - interesting and threatening. It showed a white map of Europe with boundaries in black. Then a section of Europe was blacked out - it looked like Poland - then came Hitler's photo and another section of Europe was blacked out. And so it went on until the whole of Europe disappeared into black, except a section of France. The reality of Hitler and the situation rising in Germany hit home. The irony of this, an Olympic team on its way to Germany, watching their host making threatening overtones to another community."

The Berlin Olympic Games were held from August 1st to August 16th, 1936. For the first time a relay of three thousand young runners carried the Olympic torch from Olympia to Berlin - a distance of two thousand miles, across seven countries in eleven days. No women took part, but as in ancient times, two Greek 'priestesses' lit the sacred flame!

A total of 4066 competitors from forty nine countries went to Berlin. Just 328 were women and they represented only twenty countries. There were still no new sports. A proposal for women to take part in an equestrian event was turned down by the Olympic Committee, but gymnastics, left out in 1932, returned.

## Leni Riefenstahl and 'Olympia'

The Berlin Olympics of 1936 were to be the best visually-recorded pre-war Games, and the first to be televised. The Leni Riefenstahl film 'Olympia' immortalised many of those who appeared in it, and became renowned for the studied depiction of Jesse Owens' fabulous performances amid a cauldron of Nazi supremacy and racism. With Riefenstahl's masterly use of lighting and camera techniques that were far ahead of their time, the film 'Olympia' created a moody

FOOTNOTE*Australian Prime Minister during the 1930's.

yet beautiful record of a dark time in history. In order not to interfere with the Olympic action but still to make a great film, Riefenstahl re-staged some of the action, most notably the pole vault sequence. This meant that some of the athletes became actors for a day, but *'Olympia'* remains one of the greatest records of Olympic prowess ever made and one of which several of the women featured in this book have powerful recollections.

Tilly Fleischer features extensively in the film and received a personal copy from Leni Riefenstahl for her 70th birthday in 1981. As well as showing Tilly throwing the javelin, she appears in some edits of the film chatting to Hitler:

*Tilly (right) with Adolf Hitler (IOC)*

*"Hitler congratulated me after the victory in his private box, where all the world's presidents had once sat. I was his table companion with Leni Riefenstahl at the closing banquet and he was very natural, knew a lot about sport and at the meal he ate Mixpikals (cold vegetables) and drank only water! For us in Germany the Olympic Games were a high point and unforgettable."*

For British athlete Audrey Brown, the experience of Leni Riefenstahl's filming was less glamorous:

*"Leni Riefenstahl was a bit of a nuisance to competitors at times. I remember she removed me from my chosen position before the start of the relay heats because it was just by her 'pit' on the last bend and I was blocking her view!"*

Leni Riefenstahl filmed the women's high jump and four of the Olympians who contributed to this book are shown competing in this event - Dorothy Odam (Great Britain), Elfriede Kaum (Germany), Alice Arden (USA) and Doris Carter (Australia):

*"I have seen the famous Leni Riefenstahl film and 'Carter of Australia' does appear in it. The whole eight reels of it were used all over Australia to raise funds for 'Food For Britain' throughout the war. It raised a lot of money."*

*Tilly Fleischer throwing the javelin in Berlin 1936 (IOC)*

ONE HUNDRED AND ONE

Leni Riefenstahl may not have intended this outcome for her film. After the war she was arrested for 'pro-Nazi' work and spent many years trying to clear her name. Whatever the reality of her views, her artistic ability cannot be denied, and the record of *'Olympia'* is testament to Riefenstahl's craft.

## Militarism

Riefenstahl's masterpiece clearly depicts the militarism of the Berlin Games which left a lasting impression on the women who were there.

Doris Carter:

> *"It was very obvious that Hitler was preparing for war - more than every second person wore a uniform of some sort. But we were led to believe that they were very afraid of the Russian Bear, and had to prepare to be ready for any invasion from that direction. Hitler, of course, was very cunning. He was, as we learnt later, really facing in the opposite direction, and he planned accordingly. We heard that Hitler could travel from the Reich Chancellory to the stadium via a tunnel - we walked through tunnels from the dressing rooms to the arena. All these were prepared for air raid shelters for the Berliners if needed."*

Great Britain's high jumper Dorothy Odam recalls:

> *"We woke every morning to the sound of marching feet. When I got to the window, I could see young people with shovels held like rifles over their shoulders. I learned that they were the Hitler Youth. When we went shopping we were greeted 'Guten Morgen. Heil Hitler!' We replied 'Guten Morgen. King George!'"*

Australian swimmer Pat Norton wrote in her diary:

> *"The Sports fields were guarded by Nazi SA Troopers. Their uniforms were very forbidding to see for the first time. The tunics and trousers are black, with black boots and leggings. The tunics are belted with red armbands with the Nazi swastika emblazoned on them, but it is the black helmets that add a sombre picture to this. They come low down on the forehead, level with the eyebrows, giving the wearer a sinister look. I became used to them after a while, but I did not like them. Added to this if one were to pass them (which was quite often) a snappy Nazi salute and a 'Heil Hitler'*

*would greet you. For quite a while I did not know what they were saying as they ran both words into one another, "ile 'itler."*

The women stayed in a new building which was used after the Games for students of the Reich Academy for Physical Culture. They were well chaperoned and sixteen year old Dorothy Odam's youthful charms were to be protected!

*"There were 12 of us in the women's athletic team with 3 chaperones and no other officials. I got friendly with a Danish male high jumper who asked me out. The chaperones said I could go if I let the rest of the team go too!"*

*The young Dorothy Odam with her cups (DT)*

Perhaps the chaperones were right to be cautious.

*"I don't think I did much training whilst I was waiting for my event. If anyone was jumping I just joined in. I jumped a bit, then talked to the men!"*

One shopping trip, Dorothy remembers her chaperone telling the group she was with not to go into a particular shop:

*"We were about to enter when the interpreter said 'No, no Jews.' So we all just walked in. I was given a letter from somebody in a concentration camp telling me of all the horrible things that were going on, what was happening to them, and asking me to show it to someone in England, but being rather young I showed it to my chaperone and they took it away from me."*

Dorothy looked quite troubled recalling this story, and remarked that she was just sixteen years old and knew little about politics. Pat Norton shared a similar experience of the turmoil created by the political situation for some of the competitors:

*"Jeanette Campbell, the Argentine girl, was sent a letter a couple of weeks before the Games from a man in Holland stating that his two friends had disappeared in Germany. He asked would we rally the women competitors together and demand their release or the women would boycott the opening Ceremony! She read the letter to us and*

*there was considerable discussion about what we should do. Finally, Jeanette decided it was asking too much of her and decided to let the matter drop. We had heard stories before arriving in Berlin of missing people, but what was speculation was now a reality."*

**Fellow Australian high jumper Doris Carter wrote:**

*"We did not hear any mention of concentration camps but several charming girls who worked in Friesenhaus\* whispered to us that they were afraid - they were quarter Jewish and they had heard several of their Jewish friends had disappeared. Baroness von Wangenheim was in charge of the volunteer women guides and Fraulein Waimbeir was the officer in charge of the guides who cared for us. They both said they really didn't approve of the way things were but had no option but to go along with it."*

*Jeanette Campbell (TB)*

## Accommodation

The Olympic village was about nine miles from the stadium, where women were again barred from entering. They were housed together in dormitory rooms, Fredrich-Friesen-Haus, in quarters three stories high surrounding a large court on the Reichsportfeld. Pat Norton remembers some lighter moments:

*"The 400 women were in quarters under the control of Freifrau Johanna von Wangenheim - it was probably the longest four weeks of her life! She said she had no intention of restricting the freedom of her house guests and had no prohibitive rules and regulations. Our 'Frauenheim' housed about twenty women; we shared with the South Americans, and the Japanese girls. No-one could converse with one another, except Jeanette, the Argentine, who spoke Spanish and English. With the little Japanese girls it was hopeless and we would end up with much laughing and giggling! We got by with handsigns, pointing and much laughter."*

*The 'Friesenhaus (BH)'*

FOOTNOTE\* The ladies quarters

Pat formed a friendship with Jeanette Campbell, who was to win a silver medal in the 100 metres freestyle. They got into a few scrapes:

> "'Verboten' became a very well known word in Germany. No one was allowed in the main stadium before the opening day, only tourists with their guides. Jeanette Campbell and I decided we would try to do this! We hit on the idea to mix with the tourists and when they drew opposite an entrance to the stadium we would duck in. All went to plan, we got in but not surprisingly we were chased by a Stormtrooper shouting 'Verboten! Verboten!' We did manage to run up a flight of the steps before we were caught and did see something of the stadium. He let us off when we confirmed our identity, but still said 'Verboten, Verboten!'
>
> We discovered the automat in a shop one day and had great delight in selecting our food and being served by the machine. Our popularity with 'Cookie', boss of the kitchen in Frauenheim, allowed us to sneak into the kitchen and help ourselves to a snack or two!"

Dorothy Odam remembers:

> "In those days men were more important than women in every walk of life. The woman took second place and therefore you toddled along behind. There was a special village for the men but we were in a women's PT college and never allowed in the men's village. The only time we met them was at the communal training arena, but I quite often thought I heard a man's voice behind me, only to find it was a woman! We didn't have sex tests in those days."

Once again, the issue of gender was around - but friendships were also forming. Doris Carter established important relationships with her two guides, Ingrid and Helga.

> "There was a wonderful service of honorary guides, usually young university students who spoke your language. Ingrid and Helga spent all day with us and became our friends. I corresponded with both of them after I returned home, until war made it impossible. I did not hear from Helga after the war but did receive a letter from Ingrid. She had become a doctor. Her father, whom we knew was a general, had been killed, and also her husband. I should very much have liked to track her down when I re-visited Berlin but being back in uniform (WAAF) made it too difficult. I was delighted she valued my friendship."

## Kit and Clothes

Pat Norton's new friend, Jeanette Campbell, had travelled over with the Argentine team by ship:

> "My future husband, Roberto, belonged to the same swimming club as me and we both went there and broke South American records. Roberto had gone to Los Angeles in 1932. We always trained together. We both worked in those days, so only swam a while in the evening. He was named in 1936 to go to Berlin, but the cash didn't stretch, so I had to go alone. The trip there was not so much fun, as I had to sit at table with the directors and trainers. They always had problems and were always squabbling, but when you crossed the Equator, there was always a fancy dress dinner. We dressed up, but changed sexes. I was in shorts (not worn in those days), a dinner jacket, coat and hat, and my bride was our fencer in my sister's evening dress. Not having been at the dinner very long, the Captain of the ship stood up and came over, carrying a lovely little baby doll which he placed in the fencer's lap."

Dorothy Odam remembers setting off for Berlin to compete for Great Britain in the high jump with a distinctly makeshift kit:

> "We left London by train but did not travel with the men. I was clutching a lion which was our mascot. At 16 I was very excited. I had very old spikes with my toe hanging out because I couldn't afford new ones, a pair of shorts and a top that I had to make myself. They gave me some red and blue bands to put round my top and some red, white and blue stripes to put down my shorts. We were given a cravat, dress, jacket and beret, but the rest we had to provide ourselves. It's a bit different today."

Australian Doris Carter:

> "It was rather a joke that managed to find its way into the papers, that I was sent the socks and athletic singlet meant for Les Harley, a heavy weight boxer, and he received my gear! When we made the exchange I found a male athletic singlet most unsuitable and a special top was made for me."

Violet Webb was at her second Olympic Games:

> "I had to have my spikes made for me. You couldn't go to a shop and buy them in those days. You would think they were a ton weight on your feet compared with today's ones. My father used to look after them. They've always had linseed oil on them. I've still got them now - they're not bad for 2 Olympic Games and training in between!"

The Japanese made quite an impression on Pat Down and the other Australian swimmers:

> "The Japanese uniforms were grey in colour and made the girls look drab, but when we met them at a concert one night we saw the ugly duckling turn into a swan! They came dressed in beautiful kimonos complete with obis* round their waist. What a difference dress can make - they looked delightful.
>
> One day we were at the training pool when the Japanese male swimmers arrived to train. They immediately began to undress at the poolside which made us three modest Australian girls let out a yelp and dive for cover! We were only just getting used to men wearing topless costumes. When this was explained to the Japanese trainers they undressed in the rooms provided. They wore a costume with a cord through the legs tied at the back - they were beautifully built and did not cause any offence. We continued to happily share our times together.
>
> Topless costumes caused a lot of talk in our newspapers back home, in fact our coach Harry was chosen in 1935 to model how men would look in the waist to thigh costume. One lady wrote in to the Sunday Sun and said if they all looked like Harry, why, there's no problem!"

The Olympic swimmers also had a dapper visitor to the pool. Pat explains:

> "One day in our training session at the Olympic pool our routine was livened with the arrival of a Nazi dignitary. Word went round that Hitler had come, which caused a great deal of excitement among staff and spectators. People calling out 'Heil, Heil' and giving the Nazi salute.
>
> Through the entrance came the Storm Troopers in their black uniforms forming a laneway. In swept not Hitler but Herr Göring!

FOOTNOTE* Japanese sashes

*Big, fat, rotund Herman Göring. He looked beautiful! Not in the garb of a Nazi officer, but for all the world like a country squire - immaculately tailored, jauntily hatted, and carrying a walking stick and bestowing a broad smile for all and sundry."*

## Deutsche Stadium

The site of the Deutsche Stadium, designed by Otto March and built in 1913 for the cancelled 1916 Olympics, was selected for the stadium for the 1936 Games. The new Olympic stadium was designed by March's son Werner, and was huge, oval in shape and set in the middle of 325 acres called the Reichsportfeld. Pat Norton described the landscaped grounds as 'wonderful' with over nine hundred trees creating a forest-like effect. The stadium held a hundred and ten thousand spectators in seventy two tiers of seats in upper and lower sections, which rose to forty eight feet above the sports field, and forty two feet below ground level. It allowed for very close contact with

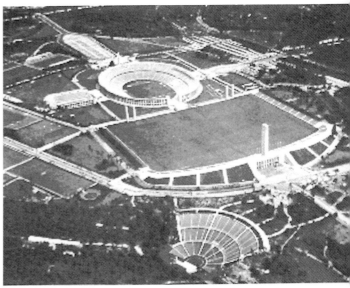

*The Reichsportfeld and the Dietrich Eckart Open Air Theatre (BH)*

contestants. The centre piece of the stadium was a specially designed ten foot high, 16.5 ton bell. It was suspended in a two hundred and forty eight foot bell tower, surrounded by fifty foot stone columns on which winners' names were carved throughout the Games. The bell, inscribed with the five Olympic rings and the words *'Citius, Altius, Fortius'* was escorted through the streets of Berlin on the way to the stadium and became the trademark for the Games. Pat remembered the bell tolling till 10 at night and machine gun fire waking the athletes at 6 in the morning. "Lack of sleep demanded the demise of the tolling and the gunfire ceased soon after that!" The names of the gold medal winners carved on the tablets of stone can still be seen, and the bell is still intact today.

## Opening Ceremony

The teams waited outside the stadium for several hours before the parade of nations began. It was a very hot day, but the uncomfortable wait was to give the teams an opportunity to meet with Chancellor Hitler. Pat Norton remembers:

*"We four girls in our team stood without rest for two hours before entering the stadium, but the air of excitement and noise among the teams drove our tiredness away. While we were making friends with the only girl in the Argentinian team of 90 men, who were standing next to us, the teams suddenly became quiet at the sight of Hitler and his entourage striding down between the teams. He looked neither to the left nor right and gave no sign of greeting or welcome. It was my first direct look at the man who was the talk of the world, and a more uninspiring-looking person would be hard to find."*

Violet Webb remarked that he seemed a smaller man than she had imagined, but her clearest impression was of Hitler's arrival in his box inside the stadium.

*"We had to wait in the polo ground for Hitler to enter - the teams were lined up either side. The diplomats came through, some countries gave the salute, but we were told not to. As he went into the stadium you would have thought God had come down from heaven."*

Dorothy Odam:

*"Before the opening ceremony there was mass hysteria when Hitler arrived in the stadium, but we had to wait for an hour in order before we could enter. It was so hot that they had to bring us refreshments."*

USA thrower Gertrude Wilhelmsen cites the march past as part of the USA team one of the most moving moments of her career:

*"My fondest memory was marching in the stadium prior to the opening ceremony in 1936."*

But fellow countrywoman and fencer, Joanna de Tuscan, remembers it quite differently:

*"When the march into the stadium was arranged we were a total disgrace. First about thirty or forty non-members of the team, fat, with cigarette ashes on their clothes, marched at the head of the team. Then came the chaperones. I had to produce my passport. I was 29 years of age and too old to march with the athletes. They made me march with the chaperones."*

The Opening Ceremony was presided over by Adolph Hitler who formally opened the Games. While the huge bell tolled, thousands of carrier pigeons were released. The airship Hindenburg flew over a stadium adorned with Olympic rings and swastikas as the German team began their march past.

Finally the 1896 marathon winner, Spyros Louis, presented Hitler with an olive branch from Olympia as a symbol of peace and friendship.

The Greek team had a single woman athlete, Domnitsa Lanitis:

*"In Berlin we Greeks were especially honoured coming from the mother country of the Olympics, but this did not make us blind to the fascist regime and the many showy majestic festivities which tried to show the world Germany's strength! I will never forget the athletic parade in the Berlin Stadium where the Greek team - as always - entered first and was saluted with great enthusiasm, and the coming into the stadium of the last torch bearer with the Olympic flame. I will never forget my emotion and pride at that moment, but I wished that it was not Hitler and his regime that had the inspiration of the Olympic torch relay!"*

*Domnitsa Lanitis, Athens 1935, hurdling at the Panhellenic Games (DC)*

Pat Norton:

*"The torch was due to arrive in the stadium at a precise time. It was only ten minutes late, a wonderful feat! It was quite a sight to see the torchbearer running into the stadium, torch held high and the flame streaming in the breeze. Standing high in the stadium, silhouetted against the skyline, he raised the torch and with a deliberate movement plunged it into the bowl. Instantly the flame flared up into the sky, and with Hitler's declaration the games were to begin."*

After the ceremony the men dispersed to the buses for transportation back to the Olympic village and the women returned to their dormitory, Friesenhaus, on foot to await their events over the next ten days.

The Deutschland Hall with room for twenty thousand people was the site for the fencing, while the gymnastic competition was held at the Dietrich-Eckhart open-air theatre on the Reichsportfeld. This was the largest open-air theatre in Germany, providing seating for another twenty thousand in three tiers of seats. It was into these sporting facilities that our 1936 Olympic women were to venture.

## Mothers at the Games!

Gertrude Wilhelmsen, discus and javelin thrower for the USA, was married with a young child when she went to the Olympics of 1936. It seems that her husband had a positive attitude to Gertie's sport:

*Gertrude and her training partner - daughter Jean! (GW)*

*"I did not realise the amount of training necessary to be really competitive, as I did not realise the importance of the Olympics. At this time I also had a daughter, two years and six months old. My husband encouraged me, and I trained in the horse and cow pasture with my husband coaching and helping out."*

In a local newspaper interview Gertie said of motherhood:

*"I'm better than I was before. I feel so free. I feel 100 per cent. Mrs Anne O'Brien (fellow US team-mate) and I would like to black the eyes of people who say that women are no good in athletics after they've had children. My physician said don't ever give it up!"*

Gertie, Anne and their supportive husbands were laying to rest those hoary myths about sport being detrimental to motherhood simply by what they were doing!

## Jesse Owens - The Emperor

All of the women who competed in 1936 and contributed to this book talk about the amazing 'Emperor' Jesse Owens, who won four gold medals in athletics. Jesse was competing in a country where the political beliefs of Hitler's Party saw him as inferior because of his colour. This ideology of Aryan supremacy was of course blown away to the four corners of the Olympic world simply by Jesse's quiet achievements. Evelyn de Lacy, Australian swimmer:

*"The memory I have of the 1936 Olympic Games is of watching Jessie Owens. I never missed any of his races, he ran with such beauty and grace, he was so beautiful to watch."*

American javelin and discus thrower, Gertrude Wilhelmsen:

*"Jessie Owens asked me to be his shuffle board partner on the ship to Berlin in 1936. I was thrilled! A green farm girl being a team mate of Jesse Owens! Jesse was my hero and I gave up a chance of meeting Hitler to see Owens compete in his events."*

Hitler's presence was a powerful one and the athletes were interested in his reaction to events. Violet Webb recalls:

> *"I was in the stadium the day Jesse won his 100 and long jump. We would automatically turn up to the box and look at Hitler to see the expression on his face."*

Italian sprinter, Fernanda Bullano has a rather personal memory of Jesse:

> *"On the day of the relay finals, it was a bit cold, I was in the underpass and he covered my legs with a blanket. At the start of his fourth gold medal race, he blew me a kiss!"*

USA high jumper Alice Arden:

> *"The German people were absolutely wonderful. Except for Hitler. He turned his back on Jessie Owens when all the medal winners were brought up to meet him, and that incensed us all."*

It has been a matter of considerable speculation as to whether or not Hitler met Jesse Owens. On her own meeting with Hitler, after her victory in the javelin, Tilly Fleischer says:

> *"I was very impressed, even fortunate at this time because he was a very famous man. Even Jesse Owens was with him, although 'liars' put it about that it was not true."*

On the first day of the Games, Hitler invited all the winners to his box and it was there that Tilly was photographed extensively with him. Hitler was not part

**The grand-daughter of Jessie Owens, Gina Hempill, carried the Olympic torch into the stadium in the 1984 Los Angeles Olympics.**

of the official medal awards ceremony and one view is that Hitler was trying to upstage the official IOC medal ceremony for his own propaganda purposes by linking himself with champion athletes.

Certainly, several Finnish and German champions (all white) made their way up to the Chancellor's box during the first afternoon of competition. As dusk fell, it rained and Hitler left his box - before the completion of the high jump and at a time when it looked certain that black American athletes Cornelius Johnson and David Albritton were going to win. Did Hitler want to avoid the rain and get home for his tea or did he want to avoid meeting and having his photograph taken with the black winners?

The next day, the IOC insisted that Hitler met with all the winners or none at all, and on August 4, 1936, the German Presidential Chancellory issued a statement:

*"As the Fuhrer and Chancellor of the Reich could not be present at all of the final competitions and were therefore unable to receive the winners of different nations, receptions of the winners after the individual finals in the Fuhrer's box will no longer take place; only German winners will be introduced to the Fuhrer in the case of his being present at the victory of a German in the final.*

*The Fuhrer and Chancellor of the Reich reserve the right to personally greet and congratulate all the winners after the Closing Ceremony of the 16 August in the hall of honour at the bell tower before his departure from the Reich's sports ground; a personal introduction will not be possible on this occasion due to the large number of winners."* 1

*Domnitsa Lanitis walking in Berlin at the 1936 Games (DC)*

Greek hurdler Domnitsa Lanitis had a first class view of events and remembers the men's long jump particularly vividly:

*"The places of the officials were next to the ones of the athletes and I followed Hitler very well.*

*What impressed me greatly was his behaviour during the famous competition of Owens, the black American, and Luz Long, the Aryan German. Hitler was following with great interest and agony and was very pleased until the last jump when Owens made the winning jump! Hitler changed colour, was furious and upset and got up and left the stadium right away!"*

Whatever the truth of the 'snub' incident, Jesse Owens and other black athletes discredited Nazi ideology simply by what they did, and Jesse's exceptional performances would still gain him international vests for many countries today. His long jump record lasted twenty five years, and his 6.6 second 60 metre sprint, forty years.

## Rie Mastenbroek - The Empress

If Jesse Owens was The Emperor, then only one woman could be Empress. The women's swimming events were dominated by the amazing figure of Wilhelmina 'Rie' Mastenbroek. Rie won three Olympic gold medals and one silver.

The Swimming Stadium for this outstanding performance had two pools, one for swimming and one for diving, with 7,600 permanent swimming seats which could be expanded to accommodate sixteen thousand spectators. Behind the thirty three foot high diving tower was a restaurant with terraces overlooking the pool, and it was here that Rie set her Olympic record in the 100 metres freestyle and won her first gold on Monday August 10th. She followed this by swimming through the preliminary rounds of the backstroke (for which she held the world record) and the 400 metres freestyle. The final of the backstroke took place on the same day as the heats of the 400, so Rie had already swum one strenuous event. She was beaten into second place by her team mate Dina Senff. On the morning of August 14th, Rie swam in the semi-final of the 400 and then, with her team mates, gained her second gold in the 4 by 100 freestyle relay.

In the 400 freestyle, Rie's main rival was Danish swimmer Ragnhild Hveger who unwittingly gave impetus to Rie's desire to win. Hveger received a large box of chocolates from her supporters and offered them around to everyone - but deliberately bypassed Rie! Rie was disappointed but went out for revenge.

For the first 350 metres of the final, Hveger and Rie swam alongside each other. Over the last fifty metres, Rie began her sprint which Hveger couldn't live with. As Rie moved ahead she thought:

*"This is much better than a piece of chocolate!"2*

Rie convincingly won her third gold medal.

*Rie Mastenbroek (Holland) centre, gold - Jeanette Campbell, (Argentina) left, silver - Gisela Arendt (Germany) right, bronze, 100 metres freestyle (TB)*

In 1986, at the fiftieth anniversary celebration of the Berlin Games, German Olympic Committee president and IOC member Willy Daume said in his speech:

> "Ladies and gentleman, as you know Jesse Owens was the Emperor of the Berlin Olympics in 1936. But there was also a young girl, she became the Empress of Berlin...." 3

He pointed to Rie who was attending the ceremony along with several other medalists. Her friend, historian Tony Bijerk, wrote that:

> "Rie Mastenbroek never really received the acclaim that she so richly deserved. Even in the Centennial Olympic year 1996, she was only interviewed by very few representatives from the Dutch media; and the international media including the Atlanta Olympic Organising Committee completely forgot her existence. She had deserved to be invited to the spectacle of the opening ceremony, together with the other ten Olympic gold medal winners." 4

It is unlikely that Rie, whose achievements were so outstanding, would have been forgotten if she had been a male Olympian.

## The Eleanor Jarrett Holm Affair

Backstroke Olympic champion from 1932, Eleanor Jarrett Holm, was never an orthodox figure. The legendary Ziegfield of the 'Follies' said that she was the most beautiful figure he had ever seen. Eleanor was a stunning beauty, media celebrity, film star and a wonderful swimmer - she also liked to party.

On the boat on the way over to Berlin, Eleanor lived her life as she had always done. She once said that she trained on champagne and not too much sleep. She was a veteran Olympian, having competed in Amsterdam in 1928 before taking gold in '32, and was an adult, married woman. This cut no ice with the American Olympic Committee when they warned Eleanor about her infractions of training rules and drinking parties on ship. She promised that she wouldn't do it again - but she just couldn't resist a champagne party with Charlie MacArthur, the playwright, and his wife Helen Hayes.

The Committee went to call Eleanor to a meeting, but she was asleep. They took drastic action and expelled her from the team, ordering her to return her blue Olympic uniform. Eleanor pleaded with them to give her a chance to tell her side of the story, which she did on the train to Berlin.

Eleanor explained that she had commonly gone to a party, then into the water to win a race. She even said that she had been out late partying with her husband the night before the Olympic trials in New York and still won! She would change from an evening gown to a swimming suit and out-swim everyone in the race. Eleanor was in tears, and told the Committee that expulsion would ruin her career - that she had been blind about the rigorous discipline imposed on the Olympic team. The Committee was unmoved and she was thrown off the team. A radio broadcast by Lowell Thomas on July 24th, 1936, said:

> *"Eleanor attended the official German reception to the American athletes. One ceremony is a glass of sherry served to each, and drunk in a formal ritual of hospitality. Every American athlete drank his or her glass of sherry - except Eleanor Holm Jarrett. She put hers aside, didn't take a sip.*

> *This affair is a bad blow to American swimming hopes in the Olympics and one cannot help thinking of Lincoln's immortal utterance when they complained to him that General Grant was drinking too much. Lincoln said he wished they'd find out what brand of whisky Grant drank because he would like to send it to his other generals."*

With the exception of the divers, the American women came nowhere near emulating their swimming performances of 1928 and '32, and the loss of Eleanor Jarrett Holm was a huge blow. It is worth reflecting on what her performances might have been if she hadn't been such a party animal, but, as Lowell Thomas put it, "Mirth and jollity were her way - not the severities of athletic training." 5

## Leisure Time

Eleanor Holm may have been sent home for her partying whilst Dorothy Odam couldn't escape her chaperones - but the athletes did have some fun in Berlin. Pat Norton:

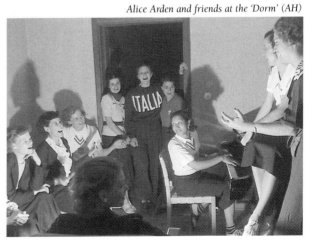

*Alice Arden and friends at the 'Dorm' (AH)*

> *"We were often escorted to open air restaurants by four good looking, heel clicking, Nazi officers for supper. The men were studiously polite and we got the impression they were there in the line of duty! The American girls didn't sit at home with nothing to do either. A bus would arrive after dinner with some of the American*

*male athletes and they would all pile in and off they'd go - even one lass with her leg in plaster wasn't going to be left behind and was gratefully carried to the bus! One night we were joined by some German girls for singing. We Australians sang in a traditional way, light and pleasant, the Japanese with sweet nasally tinklings, and the Germans finished the night with robust marching songs."*

## Olympic Oaks

In addition to a gold medal, the Olympic Organising Committee presented to the winners of each event a wreath of oak leaves and a small oak tree with the inscription : 'Grow to the honour of victory! Summon to further achievement!' Three of the women in this book received these oak seedlings, gifts of the German people to be taken home and planted as a gesture of goodwill and peace. Tilly Fleischer had won a bronze medal in Los Angeles in 1932 in the javelin, but went on to top it with a gold in Berlin:

*"My oak from 1936 died in Autumn 1998. However, I immediately planted a new one. It stands in the Frankfurt Stadium with a shield 'Olympic Oak, Tilly Fleischer'."* 6

British athlete Audrey Brown won a silver medal in the relay. Silver medalists were rewarded with laurel wreaths:

*"Standing on the rostrum with the Canadians and Americans and looking round the vast stadium from this exciting point was the most important moment of the Games for me, despite wearing rather ridiculous oakleaf laurels!"*

Audrey had a problem quite separate from wearing her laurel wreaths:

*"I was always nervous at the start of a race because of my considerable deafness and fear of not hearing starters orders. My hearing difficulty was not a severe one - just an inconvenience - but I found I could not relax sufficiently to be assured of a good start. In those days very little was available in the way of help for the deaf and one did not speak about it but just adapted as best one could. People are more positive about disabilities now I am thankful to say."*

It is paramount in sprint events to get a good start - it is worth speculating how much quicker Audrey's times might have been had there been a visual cue for her at the start.

## Snapshots of the Games - Glory and Disappointment

### Gertie Wilhelmsen, USA (Javelin and Discus)

*"I was given no opportunity to warm up before my event and had no opportunity to train or practise. It was a thrill for me just to be there. I was placed 7th in discus and 9th in javelin, but I did better than the other US girls in these events."*

### Tilly Fleischer, Germany (Javelin)

*"In the javelin competition at the Olympics there was an American who was ready to take her throw when I noticed that she was holding the javelin the wrong way round. I quickly let her know and turned the spear round for her! She was very grateful. I won it with an Olympic record. I also remember a British team official from Berlin 1936, Mr Preston. He had badly fitted teeth and when he spoke they rattled and this amused the British and German team members!"*

### Audrey Brown, Great Britain (100 metres and 4 by 100 relay)

*Frl Dollinger and Frl Dorfeld (Germany) drop the baton in the relay, Audrey Brown (inside lane) hands over the baton and gets silver (UF)*

*"My effort in the 100 metres was ruined by the fact that at the last moment I was moved out of my lane where I had already 'dug' my starting holes to fit my small feet and into the next inner one, which was empty, where I found enormous 'pits' dug by the very large and mannish ******, and was given insufficient time to fill in and re-dig my own! Our feelings that women athletes, particularly non-German ones,*

*After the relay, Kathe Kraus gets consolation (UF)*

were a lesser breed were well borne out! The 4 by 100 relay for women was to be one of their key successes and Hitler himself was to present the Gold medal, but the superbly drilled German team unbelievably dropped the baton with highly emotional results. I have often wondered whether the Germans would have won the relay and I think the Germans felt this pressure themselves. Helen Stephens, the American individual 100 metres winner, was such an unknown quantity, running faster and faster each time she went out. Fortunately we managed to keep our heads and came in a creditable second. Hitler did not present the medals, instead he consoled the German quartet in his box in the stands."

Audrey ran the third leg for the British team who won the silver medal in the relay, and she was thrilled to watch brother Godfrey win silver in the individual 400 metres and gold in the relay.

## Doris Carter, Australia (High Jump)

*Doris Carter (CD, JC)*

"The team of 33 members consisted of 4 women - 3 swimmers and me. We six athletes were disappointed with our performances. We all had injuries, were performing out of season, after a long voyage, and encountered cinder tracks for the first time in our lives. We trained so hard on this new surface to get accustomed to it, that we all had strains and sprains. Our pole-vaulter, Fred Woodhouse, could not even compete. I finished 6th equal with Fanny Blankers-Koen (Holland) and Annette Rogers (USA)."

## Dorothy Odam, Great Britain (High Jump)

*Dorothy in action (DT)*

"*Most people have nerves and get in a state in competition. The women's high jump wasn't until the last day. I was getting fed up not getting out there. I wanted to get out and perform. I didn't fail at all until the final jump which we all failed, but I got over the one before on my first jump, which today would have given me the gold medal. In those days, they lowered the bar a quarter of an inch and you all tried. We all jumped it. They raised it, we all jumped, then lower, then higher, and the Hungarian girl cleared it. The German girl dropped out before then. During the actual competition, which lasted for three hours, there was an awful lot of cheering for the German girl and she was allowed a drink during the competition, which we weren't. The only people cheering for me were a crowd of British scouts! In the end, I won silver, though I jumped the same height as the winner. Lord Aberdare presented the medal in a box in the stadium.*"

*Elfriede Kaun (ERK)*

*The high jump medal ceremony, Elfriede Kaun (Germany 3rd), Ibolya Csak (Hungary 1st) Dorothy Odam (Great Britain 2nd) (IOC)*

## Violet Webb, Great Britain (80 metres Hurdles)

"*In my semi-final of the hurdles I think I was unfortunate. I had the 1, 2, and 3 in my heat who came 1, 2, 3 in the final. So I didn't make it. No new shoes, the same old shoes! It used to be cinder tracks and we used to dig a hole for our feet. If you compare the times we ran and the conditions, we didn't do so badly really.*"

## Pat Norton, Australia (100 metres backstroke)

In her eloquent writing, Pat clearly describes the difficulties the Australians faced after their long journey, to be confronted by conditions and standards very different from those they were used to - and also the effect that 'unmentionable' menstruation had on women swimmers.

*"We didn't do well at the Games. Only Evelyn de Lacy did a personal best. Our times and results were disappointing but the shock of the Games was the amount of training done by the competitors of other teams! It was the same for athletics and swimming. My training schedule amounted at most to six to eight hundred metres a day. This was considered highly trained. Last season I had clocked up 30,000 yards and felt that was quite impressive, but these swimmers were doing that much in a week!*

*At this stage our coach, Harry Nightingale, was reluctant to suddenly increase our training schedule, as he felt we were not conditioned to it. A newspaper article had warned my coach the previous summer to be careful and not overload me with work, otherwise I might get burned out! The athletes were shocked to find themselves running on cinder tracks, none in Australia. They ran on grass, much softer on the muscles than cinders, which caused a number of leg injuries, bruised heels, strained and sore muscles. Doris Carter, our high jumper, fell a victim to this and went into her event untrained.*

*The Dutch girls were the outstanding swimmers at the Games but a shock second place in the 100 metres freestyle by the Argentine girl, Jeanette Campbell, stopped their run of all three places. The American divers were wonderful, they trained for hours and they had a finish to their diving which outclassed all others.*

*My effort in the 100 metres backstroke was abysmal. It was a great disappointment to me. Losing a week's training with a swollen gland, then to be confronted with my period on the day of the race did nothing for my morale. Menstruation was not a subject for general discussion among us girls ourselves, let alone with a male swimming coach! I was lethargic and slightly depressed and my limbs felt as if they had turned to lead. I managed to make the semi-final, but if I had repeated my Australian record I would have come third. Well, these things happen, and you only have one chance and that's that."*

For most of the women at these games, it was to be their only shot at an Olympic title, for World War II deprived many a future opportunity.

## Gymnastics

For the first time in the history of the Olympics the gymnastics events were held in a Stadium outside, where canvas shelter was provided in case of rain. Great Britain's team gymnast member Edna Gross recalled:

> "Gymnastics was not performed in the main stadium but in the Dietrich Eckart open-air theatre. This was the first time our team had performed in the open air."

Swedish women gymnasts first gave two displays using portable apparatus on Saturday 8th August and Germany a third on Sunday 9th. The following day the Olympic Gymnastic competition began. It was strictly a team affair.

Women from eight nations with teams of eight gymnasts took part. Their event with parallel bars, balance beam, side horse vault, compulsory and optional exercise, and two optional team drills (one free hand and one with hand apparatus) lasted all day. Team drill exercises showed the different kinds of physical training each country favoured. The Germans and Czechs were experimenting with new and innovative styles and the introduction of the asymetrical bars was exciting - even though the British women had never seen such apparatus! In the individual work the six best on each piece of apparatus counted for their team total.

*Edna Gross (GB) on balance beam (MW, ME)*

Trudi Meyer scored the highest total individual mark of **67.5** and came in first helping her team to win the gold medal for Germany.

> "It was a pleasure for me to do sports and to compete. I also had a coach who helped me a lot and on 12/8/36 I attained the Best in the World Gold Medallion with the team. To my joy my future husband, whose birthday was on the same day, was able to experience the world competition with me."

*Trudi Meyer (Germany) gold medal team gymnastics with her husband (TB)*

*German gold medal gymnastic team (IOC)*

**XI. OLYMPIADE BERLIN 1936**

FRAUENHEIM

OLYMPIA AUSWEIS

*Brenda's Olympic pass (BH)*

It had been decided at the last moment to send the British women's team to Berlin instead of the men. The men's team had been in training and expecting to go, but were thought not to be of sufficient standard. Edna Gross remembers wryly:

*"As usual our country was short of money, so it was decided to send only a men's team to the Olympic Games. Just six weeks before leaving England the Association decided the men couldn't cope with the set exercises so it was decided to train up the women! I had only been married three months so cried copiously when we set off. Soon cheered up, particularly meeting up with some of the athletes."*

Brenda Crowe described the invitation to attend the Berlin Games as "a bit of a shock," and thought "Heavens! What have I let myself in for?"

She remembered that the newspapers of the time had some interesting comments to make:

*"Just before we left a newspaper wrote: 'Amazons train on porridge. Cream buns and chocolate are not barred, but smoking is. Britain's gymnasts reveal their secrets'."*

As the tallest of the team was only 5 feet 4 inches tall, the women gymnasts understandingly did not like to be referred to as 'amazons'! While most of the women in the Berlin Games wore shorts, the team of British gymnasts were dressed in skirts and long stockings. This was the regulation dress for women in the Amateur Gymnastics Association. Officials considered that short dresses were more graceful and becoming than the shorts worn by women athletes. Looking 'feminine' was still a priority.

The Amateur Gymnastic Association thought that the British team was disadvantaged - not by the skirts, but because they were drawn to compete first in each event and because a new style of work on parallel bars had been decided upon for the Olympic competition. This information came too late, they

thought, and wrote in their Olympic report that "they would have come higher up the list if they had been given the compulsory or published exercises sooner, leaving more time to practise." This fact would surely have applied to all competing teams. Brenda Crowe described the German team as "excellent" and felt rather awed by their extraordinary level of performance. The British team had trained hard but at the end of an exciting competition Germany won the gold, with Czechoslovakia taking silver and Hungary the bronze.

*Brenda in gym pose showing a neighbour how she performed in the Games! (BH)*

## Fencing

There was just one fencing competition for women - the individual foil. The matches were held in the large gymnasium and were popular and well attended. But Ilona Elek's win for Hungary was overshadowed by the publicity given to Helene Mayer.

Helene Mayer had competed for Germany as a fencer in Amsterdam in 1928 and won the gold medal. She was world foil champion in 1929 and 1931 and competed in the Los Angeles Olympic Games of 1932. Helene decided to study law in Los Angeles and stayed there after the Games. In 1933, she learned that she had been expelled from her club, Offenbach Fencing Club. Her expulsion coincided with the implementation of Hitler's racist policies. Helene had a Christian mother and a Jewish father.

To appease those who cited Hitler's racist policies as a reason to stage the Olympic Games elsewhere, the Germans invited Helene Mayer to fence for them again in 1936, and she was declared an Aryan by the German government. In spite of her expulsion from her club, she agreed. She went on to win the silver medal and, to the surprise of many, gave the Nazi salute on the winner's podium. Ironically the winner, Ilona Elek, from Hungary, who also won the gold medal in 1948, was Jewish. Ellen Preis (Austria), the champion of 1932, won bronze.

*The de Tuscan foil (invented 1939) (MF)*

The Captain of the USA women's fencing team, Joanna de Tuscan, did not have the best of Games:

*"I fenced with an Italian foil. It was the only weapon and method that ever won, but the official coach on the ship used the French foil and he made me train with him with French foil, on a rocking ship. I objected and so did another coach, but to no avail. I landed in Berlin totally stale."*

Joanna struggled in her competitions with the French foil, but her good looks attracted the German press and the Fuhrer.

*"On the trip to Germany to the Olympics they had a beauty contest. I paid very little attention to it and was in my stateroom when they announced the winner. There was a knock on my door and I was truly surprised when I was voted the most beautiful Olympian! When I arrived in Germany I received a lot of publicity and headlines read 'Sports macht nicht hastik' (Sports do not make you ugly). Hitler was trying to promote a female army and I had so much publicity that Hitler had his first lieutenant escort me to the most spectacular parties and meetings. He took me everywhere by back routes as the public wanted my autograph!"*

Training on board ship in those pre-aeroplane days for any Olympic event was never an easy task, but training on the long Atlantic journey to Berlin for the American fencing competitors must have been exceptionally hazardous!

*Joanna de Tuscan (MF)*

# The Party After the Games

The closing ceremony on August 16th was witnessed by a crowd of 110,000 spectators in the Stadium after the final exciting equestrian event, the Team Grand Prix (Jumping). The Germans had already won all five gold medals in equestrian events, and the crowd were not denied the clean sweep and a place in equestrian history with the sixth and final German victory. After the last Olympic medal was presented, Count Baillet-Latour, the IOC President, called for the world's youth to meet in 1940 in Tokyo. The moment is etched into Pat Down's memory:

> "The games finished and we thought no more until 1940, Japan! The Closing Ceremony had a sad ring to it, as the flags of all the Nations were marched round the arena accompanied by the sound of rolling guns firing, followed by a choir singing 'Song of the Flags'. It was saying goodbye to the friends we made at Frauenheim that saddened us. Jeanette from the Argentine, who just waved 'goodbye' and did not look back, our giggly little Japanese girls and South Americans. Somehow it didn't seem right - we were very subdued realising we would never see them again."

A dinner party was later organised for the competitors and it was here that Tilly Fleischer sat at the top table with Leni Riefenstahl and Hitler, who ate only vegetables and drank only water and seemed very 'natural'. Many of the Olympians have their invitations to this day.

Dorothy Odam remembers that the dinner was held on an island:

> "It was beautiful. The whole island was lit up by lanterns. We crossed over on pontoons managed by soldiers. I was awe-struck. All the crown heads of Europe were there and being able to walk past Goebbels, Goering and Hitler! For a sixteen year old...yet no-one was interested when I got back."

Dorothy sadly recalled that just a few neighbours had asked her how she had got on when she returned home. She went on to set a new world high jump record in 1939 - the year World War II broke out. For all the competitors the outbreak of the war had a particular poignancy. Violet Webb:

> "I cannot describe the war to anybody. When I opened my door and it was red, that was London burning. The fires were dreadful in London and after that we had the doodle bugs. London was burning.

*It was terrifying. I could still see these people at the games and now they were bombing us. He must have been planning it in 1936."*

In Germany, Tilly Fleischer worked on her grandparents land near Frankfurt:

*"In October 1944 we were bombed and nearly everything was destroyed. We were evacuated to Halle, but my husband came and brought the children and I back to our grandparents just before the Russians arrived. In April 1945, our village was occupied by twenty Americans who cooked up ham and eggs before moving east"*

After the war, Australian Doris Carter returned to Berlin:

*"In 1946 I re-visited the Reichsportfeld. The stadium was little damaged but other buildings were wrecked. Trees and window frames had been burnt for firewood. What was left of the Bell Tower that called the 'youth of the world' to the Games contained damaged machinery that I imagine provided the air conditioning for all those tunnels."*

All the athletes at the Olympic Games of 1936 were in the presence of a figure who has been described as the most evil man in history and some were even asked to take action on behalf of his victims. If Jeanette Campbell and her fellow swimmers had refused to march in the Opening Ceremony, or had Dorothy Odam been able to take the letter passed on to her to a British politician, instead of her chaperone confiscating it, would the outcome have been any different?

Athletes competing in countries where the political or religious systems are different from their own are constantly faced with situations that challenge their consciences. Sport does not exist in a vacuum. Brenda Crowe summed things up:

*"I remember one of the men was appalled by the stories he was hearing, but we thought it just had to be exaggerated and you just have to put it behind you."*

# Chapter 9 - Where to Next?

The first official woman Olympian, Helen de Pourtales, sailed into the history books in 1900 without even knowing her significance. By the time the sun had set over the closing ceremony at Berlin in 1936, women had travelled a very long way - but the journey was far from over.

Since World War II, the number of sports and events for women has slowly increased and at the Atlanta Olympics of 1996 three thousand six hundred and twenty six women took part, 40% of the total number of competitors that year. Looking back to the few women - one hundred and twenty seven - who went to the Los Angeles Games of 1932 we are sharply reminded how unique the experience was of those women featured in this book. Yet there are still places in the world where cultural traditions, 'old-fashioned' attitudes, and social difficulties preserve gender inequality. In some Islamic countries, women athletes attempting to train have been stoned in the street.

Perhaps one of the most exciting developments in Olympic sports during the 1980s and 90s has been the emergence of African and Muslim women athletes. Nawal El Moutawakel-Bennis, Moroccan Olympic 400 metres hurdles gold medalist in 1984, herself an IOC member, wrote:

> *"...the appearance of an African woman athlete on the international scene must be regarded as a miracle, because her success involves the whole gamut of sacrifice, challenge and courage."*[1]

When survival is dependant on meeting the basic needs of food, education and health it is not surprising, but sad, that sport for girls and women remains relatively unimportant. At the Olympic Games in Atlanta in 1996, the Olympic Committees of twenty six countries sent no female participants. It would seem that sporting women in developing countries continually have to challenge negative social attitudes - a struggle similar to that of women in the 'developed' world a century ago.

The standard of performance in women's sports after World War II has risen dramatically. Statistical analysis shows that the comparative improvement women athletes have made since 1956 is much greater and more pronounced than that made by male athletes during the same period - yet media interest mainly remains focused on male sport.

There have been other difficulties for women. In the 1960s, gender testing was introduced, involving a basic physical examination. Some women athletes subjected to these examinations have later described their experiences as verging on the abusive. Gender testing remains a murky, confused area, with definitions of femaleness remaining open to debate.

Within the hallowed male offices of the International Olympic Committee, the pace of change has been snail-like. An influential and controversial female figure emerged during the 1960s - Madame Monique Berlioux. French champion and Olympic swimmer, Monique Berlioux was never elected an IOC Member but worked with three IOC Presidents - Avery Brundage, Lord Kilannin and Juan Antonio Samaranch. Working as a Director of the IOC from 1969 - though she was not dignified with the official title until 1971 - she said retrospectively:

*"They tried to find a man, of course, but they could not find the right person for months and months, so I continued to do the job. After two years I said, 'If you don't intend to nominate someone else you could ratify me.' "* [2]

*Monique Berlioux (MB)*

Monique worked for the IOC for many years, but rumours of bitter disagreements surrounded her resignation in 1985. In a letter she wrote:

*"My best Olympic memory was 15th August 1939, when I was told I would compete in the 1940\* Games. My worst was 6th June 1985 when I left the IOC. I did not like the way things were going within Olympism."* [3]

Whatever friends or enemies Madame Berlioux made during her time with the IOC, it cannot be denied that she strove relentlessly to encourage everyone - male and female - to fight for women to be present everywhere in sporting bodies.

It was under the current presidency of Juan Antonio Samaranch that Monique Berlioux resigned, but it is during Samaranch's presidency that women have at last become members of the IOC. President Samaranch has had a troubled period in office dealing with allegations of corruption within the IOC. The increasing influence of money in Olympic sport has, as in the Ancient Games, lead to cheating and the use of

\*FOOTNOTE Madame Berlioux was another athlete to miss out on Olympic competition during World War II

performance-enhancing drugs amongst some athletes. Although presiding during a difficult time for the Olympic movement, Samaranch has supported the setting of targets within the 'Olympic family' to establish women in 10% of legislative and executive positions by the year 2000, and 20% by 2005.

Looking back a hundred years, what would Baron Pierre de Coubertin make of his successor Juan Antonio Samaranch and current IOC Vice President, Anita DeFrantz? Olympic rowing medalist in 1976, a lawyer and a black woman, Ms DeFrantz fought the American boycott of the Moscow Games of 1980. She was elected to the IOC in 1986, rose to the Executive Board in 1992 and became one of the four Vice Presidents in 1997.

While she was Chair of the IOC Working Group on Women and Sport, we asked her what difficulties she felt women faced. She replied:

*"I have to say that to me it is like being a member of any group with a goal to accomplish. I don't view things as 'difficulties.' I view things as challenges. I am confident that we will be able to meet those challenges."* 4

*Anita DeFrantz (IOC)*

It is this kind of determination that has sustained so many of the brave women who have ensured that women in the Olympic Games are **'A Proper Spectacle'** and a great deal more.

## After the Games

Anita DeFrantz has gone on to even greater achievement following her career as an Olympic competitor. But she was fortunate enough to pursue her sporting career at a time in the 1970s when things were beginning to change again for women, largely as a result of the influence of the Women's Liberation Movement.

The women whose careers we have chronicled in this book were born in a different age, long before Women's Liberation became the mass movement which opened doors for so many women in all walks of life. The idea of challenging the male hierarchy of the International Olympic Committee and demanding a place in its ranks would have been inconceivable to most of them. Thus their achievements since competing in the Games have largely been quieter and less dramatic - the achievements of motherhood and raising families. Yet many in their own way have also managed to give much back to the sports that they loved.

It cannot be easy to settle back into ordinary life after the experience of competing at an Olympic Games. The heightened emotional charge of competition combined with the dramas and friendships quickly formed, and often as quickly lost, sometimes made returning to normal routine difficult. What happened to our pioneers in the years after they came together for a couple of extraordinary weeks in their lives? Many of them wrote to us to update their stories, and we include their views on what it might be like to compete again as young women today.

Very sadly, several women we were in touch with died whilst this book was being completed - Leni Thymm Junker, Wilhelmina Kuyper Duchateau, Betty Schwartz Robinson, Edna Gross Earl, Carol Metten Fletcher, Doris Carter and Violet Simpson Webb. We would particularly like to thank their families for their help.

(The married names of the women in this chapter have been added as prefixes in accordance with some European custom.)

## Family Life

For most of the women who competed in the early years of this century, their next goal was to be marriage and motherhood - and for many that was to spell the end of their sporting careers, though most continued to pursue sport as a hobby.

*Jean Burnett McDowell (left) and Sarah (Cissie) Hunt Stewart reunited in 1998 (SD, AT)*

*"You got married and you looked after your husband and children and you didn't gad about. That was typical of the time. I had to give up my job in the Civil Service - that was just how it was."*

**Jean Burnett McDowell**, one of the three British swimmers whose personal drama unfolded in Amsterdam in 1928, does not resent having left the limelight. For world class athletes today there are business opportunities in the media and advertising. They are invited to appear on television in quiz shows or to write biographies of their lives. It was a very different story for the athletes of the 1920s. As Jean's team-mate Cissie Hunt Stewart told us, "things changed when you got married."

Cissie's own romantic story created a few headlines at the time. She caused a shock at the Empire Games in Canada in 1934 when she ran off and married her journalist boyfriend. Cissie knew her father would disapprove, so she took matters into her own hands and tied the knot in secret in a small town church outside Hamilton. She returned with her husband to Canada and renewed their vows some fifty years later.

Like Jean, Cissie is philosophical about her brief period of glory. Yet she does have some regrets:

> *"I'm sorry I didn't keep up with all the people I knew. There's a whole lot of things I wished I'd kept - my Olympic blazer, for example. I was very easy going and didn't realise the importance of it. It was really something to get to the Olympic Games. Seeing all these great swimmers and feeling the fellowship. It was a great feeling to me. I don't know if they have that today."*

Cissie still regularly swims thirty lengths at her local swimming baths, although she is now well into her eighties.

Sport has also continued to play a large part in Jean's life. She was hugely successful as a golfer, with a best handicap of six. She went on to become Secretary of the Ladies Golf Association in Scotland, and was made an Honorary Member of both North Berwick and Gullane Golf Clubs - yet she still poignantly recalls her time in Amsterdam, when fate robbed her of a medal:

> *"These things that happened to me in the Olympic Games disappointed me certainly. There was a lot of feeling about it. But it was a long time ago and you get over these things."*

Jean still drives her car, and lives in North Berwick in a beautiful house overlooking Bass Rock.

The third member of the team, **Joyce Badcock Cooper**, lives in a nursing home in Chichester, England, and although a little frail, enjoys managing her own financial affairs. She maintains a lively and mischievous sense of humour and is still prepared to demonstrate the niceties of freestyle arm movements to visitors. As a 'star' swimmer, Joyce in her prime was invited to swim all over the world and travelled to South Africa and Australia. Joyce's husband, John

*Joyce Badcock Cooper (SD, AT)*

Badcock, was an Olympic gold medalist rower, and her two sons also represented England as rowers. A keen spectator at Henley Regatta for many years, her love of water never abated.

In 1998, Joyce was inducted into the Fort Lauderdale Swimming Hall of Fame, yet remains incredibly modest about her achievements. Joyce's husband and two young sons meant everything to her, but may have deprived the swimming world of even greater things:

> *"I started going up to train with Howcroft, and two French girls in the swimming world said that it was criminal, and that I was swimming much faster than I had ever done. I would have liked to have found out, but it wasn't worth pleasing myself and upsetting my husband - I knew he didn't like it."*

As one of the world's greatest swimmers, her true world record potential may never have been reached. For Joyce, as for other women of her era, it was more important to care for the needs of others than to prioritise her own ambitions. Joyce always keenly guarded her amateur status and has strong views about sport today:

*"I enjoyed my swimming days and I am grateful to have been competing at a true amateur time, without drugs and commercialism. It would be impossible to get to the top now without help and I could never have coped with all the training that they do now."*

The three surviving women from the Olympics of 1924 all married and had families. Dutch swimmer **Marie Smit Vierdag's** husband died early in 1951, so she had to work to support herself and her daughter. She became a teacher, physiotherapist and her experience as an Olympic swimmer was invaluable when at the age of 65 she became an inspector of swimming in schools in Amsterdam. Life could have become difficult for Marie when she lost her sight at the age of 71 but undeterred she learned new skills:

*Marie Smit Vierdag (MSV)*

> *"I read about swimming now in braille, but I don't know any of the younger ones. The older ones keep in touch and meet a couple of*

*times a year. I also listen to the radio and the TV, sing in a choir, go to concerts, walk, take the tram and metro, my ears are very good, so I am not doing too bad! I don't swim now, though. The water hurts my eyes - the chemicals - and the doctor says I shouldn't have it in my eyes so I don't swim."*

**Signe Engdahl Johannson**, who dived at the Paris Games, married one of Sweden's top sprinters, and she maintains a keen interest in sports:

*"I have not been a 'megastar' in any of the sports I took an active part in, but I'm convinced that sport is very important in our lives when it comes to health, well being and friendship - not only for young people but also for the elderly. Still at 94 years I seldom miss a sports programme on television, radio or newspapers. So I have a good time. When Arsenal play football I take out their red and white scarf, a gift from my son many years ago."*

After American **Carol Metten Fletcher** died, her son Carl wrote:

*"My mother's Olympic experience was certainly one of the top highlights of her life. She tried to compete again in the 1932 Olympics held in Los Angeles but the Pasadena City Schools where she ended up teaching for forty years would not let her off to train or compete prior to the Games. She really was an equity feminist before her time, who did what she wanted to do."*

*Mien Kuyper Duchateau (MKD)*

**Wilhelmina Kuyper Duchateau** had a great sporting career after the Olympics as a hockey player and worked as a bi-lingual secretary for Shell. She gave up work after she got married and shared a great love of hiking with her husband. Mien never had children but was like a mother to her nephew, Bill, who lost both his parents when he was young. She died on April 28th 1999 and Bill uses similar words to those of Carl Metten in describing his mother - a 'very strong personality who lived her life her way.'

Other women of 1928 had mixed fortunes. Betty Schwartz Robinson, first ever track and field medalist, wrote to us about her love of running and the exciting people that she met. In reply to a question about whether or not she felt recognised for her achievements, Betty said, "I had some recognition of my achievements on occasions by certain individuals or organisations." She seemed particularly pleased to have known two Tarzans - Johnny Weismuller and Buster Crabbe. Both men became high profile film stars as a result of their Olympic endeavours, yet Betty was never considered for the part of Jane to Weismuller's Tarzan, let alone offered a role as a female Tarzan in her own right. After this first round of correspondence Betty became ill and her son Rick wrote to us saying:

*"Mom recovered from a near fatal airplane crash, where she survived coma, smashed body, a pin in her shorter leg, and warnings that she would not walk right, to gain a medal for the 1936 4x100 relay team, then, unable to crouch, take a second gold.... then at 85, run her segment of the Torch Relay for Atlanta - great stuff for a movie.*

*She doesn't sell her autograph, though the recipients of some often do. Some day we hope her story, her possession of greatest value, brings her something for the end of her rainbow."*

It was sad to hear that Betty died on May 18th 1999 - only those very close to Betty will know what her great story brought her. Betty Robinson's life is the stuff of fairy tales but, as with so many exceptional women, her 'Chariots of Fire' remains untold.

**Edith Payne Robinson** corresponds regularly and lives on her own, though she says it is not easy for her now. Edith was an athletics official for some years, and was also a keen crown green bowler. She lives at the back of the Sydney Olympic Stadium in Homebush and has watched it being built. She still does her own shopping on a scooter but says that her housework isn't what it was! Edith seems somewhat bemused by the interest now being shown in her:

*Edith Robinson in Sydney Park (EP)*

*"It is only the last four years I have had any recognition as an Olympian. It is funny now after all these years they have discovered I still exist. I have been forgotten for so long, so I am*

*going to enjoy what I can! Our athletes today are treated with kid gloves compared with the way we had to struggle. I get a few invitations, and my granddaughter takes me everywhere. She has put me down to carry the torch which will go to all Australia starting somewhere in June next year!"*

Fellow Australian **Bonnie Johnson Mealing**, who has recently become a great grandmother, says that she is unlikely to take a turn with the torch in Australia at the 2000 Games. Bonnie has however been inducted into the Hall of Champions at the Olympic Boulevard in Sydney. Looking back on her life she says:

*"My greatest achievement was winning the silver at Los Angeles and my two world records."*

Sweden's **Maud Nørklit Sundberg** competed in all kinds of sports and took part in the Veteran's World Games in Toronto in 1975, in Melbourne, Australia, in 1987 (where she won a silver medal) and in Japan in 1990. She is frustrated about her left hip getting worn out and says, "I suppose no more hurdling or tennis is possible!"

At the Veteran Games, Maud ran in the 100 metres, remarking that she was struggling with her hurdling technique by 1990! She also has a great love of music and has a clear philosophy about life:

*"In my private life I had another help by playing the piano. I started to play at age 8 and had wanted to become a concert pianist. Different circumstances made it only a dream, but at least after my divorce I became a piano teacher, in which position I worked for twenty years. I play almost everyday, giving me great pleasure. Through all the years I have taken part in a lot of gymnastics, jazz dance and, in wintertime, long walks into the forest. Still I think it is the best way to keep the body fresh and the soul in harmony."*

*Maud Nørklit Sundberg the Singer! (MN)*

Fellow sprinter from 1928, Italian **Mathilde Moraschi**, fervently says 'It's about time Olympic women were talked about' and tells of an Italian newspaper which, after the Atlanta Olympics of 1996, suggested that the opening line of the National Anthem of Italy should be re-written to change 'Brothers of Italy' to 'Sisters of Italy' because the women were so much more successful than the men! Mathilde described her sporting life after the Games:

*"I practised various disciplines for 15 years, but nothing in particular happened. They were just soap bubbles, pretty, colourful, fun, but which came to nothing. Taking part in the Olympics was the peak of my achievements. I knew the history of the Olympic Games and I was proud to be able to take part in such an event."*

Mathilde's team mate, **Vittorina Vivenza Devoti**, met her husband just after she had been selected to go to the 1932 Los Angeles Olympics, so at nineteen, she declined to make the trip. Vittorina had nine children and a very active sporting life which she describes as 'wonderful'. As do so many of the early women Olympians, Vittorina remembers the friendships she made during her athletic past. She says:

*"The Olympics was, for me, the greatest experience of my life. I competed with black and white girls of all nationalities and there was great camaraderie. Now I have the beauty of my eighty seven years!"*

**Leni Thymm Junker** was another athlete from 1928, who sadly died during the preparation of this book:

*"After the Games in 1928 nothing changed, as there was negative press coverage. I even considered giving up the sport.*

*Women had every right to participate in sport but in those days the media considered competitive sport to be harmful to women. Sport was only for fun."*

Although she had thought of giving up sport, Leni met her husband through athletics and her daughter, Hilke, remains immensely proud of her mother's achievements. Leni passed away on February 9th 1997.

The Canadian bronze medalist from 1932, **Eva Spinks Dawes**, met and married an Englishman in 1935 and has lived near the palace of Hampton Court in England for many years. Today, she seems bemused by all the fuss caused by her unauthorised trip to Russia and a

*Eva Spinks Dawes (ED)*

little cross about many of the newspaper articles in her scrap book that attribute words to her that she never uttered. Her trips to Russia and planned excursion to the Workers' Olympics in Barcelona were, to Eva, opportunities to see the world without the restrictive attention of the Canadian Athletics Federation. She seems surprised that her motivations might have been seen to be political. Eva's main interest has been her family and the various handicrafts she has mastered, and she is as proud of the awards she has for her knitting as she is her Olympic bronze medal!

**Violet Simpson Webb**, one of the team that brought home the very first Olympic athletics medal for Great Britain's women, was exceedingly proud of her athletics achievements, but even prouder of those of her daughter, Janet. Vi and her husband Harry had two daughters, Susan and Janet. Whilst Susan went on to work in the media, Janet, like Vi, had been trained in athletics in her childhood by her father. Vi clearly remembered Janet's early interest:

*"All my cups were pushed under the stairs during the war, out of the way. I brought them out to show her and she said, 'I'm going to do better than you, Mummy.' I thought 'Good for you.' And she did."*

Janet took part in three Olympics, and mother and daughter competed in seven Olympic finals between them, both winning bronze in the relay. Vi was an accomplished painter, and she shared a love of Fine Art with Harry until he died. She retired from athletics after the Berlin Games, but always maintained her passion for sport via the television and was a 'keep-fit' enthusiast all her life.

*Helen Carroll Johns carries the Atlanta bound Olympic Torch in 1996 (HCJ)*

## Fame and Friendships

Olympic friendships often endure, and those links are often strongest in the countries which seem to most value the contribution made by their ex-athletes. There must have been many tearful reunions at the Atlanta Games in 1996, when former US athletes came out of retirement to carry the Olympic flame on its journey to the stadium.

Among them was gold medal swimmer, **Helen Carroll Johns**. The handful of women who went to Los Angeles in 1932 had experienced a potent mix of economic depression and Hollywood razzmatazz. For Helen, life changed forever from that moment. Her home city of Melford, Massachusetts, laid on a great reception and she was invited to make speeches and sign autographs. Helen carried on swimming and also embarked on an academic life - gaining a BA in psychology and economics and later a Masters Degree in Education. Helen spent several years as a housewife whilst she raised her two daughters and then went on to teach disabled people. She thoroughly enjoyed carrying the Olympic torch on part of its journey to Atlanta and has strong views about the Games today:

> *"I deplore the influence of money and drugs on the Games and I am glad I am not competing. In 1999 I am now eighty five, health quite good, and I am active in several organisations. I walk, read, garden some and I live in my own home. I am trying to stay there instead of living in a retirement home. I still swim today at the YMCA. At each Olympic year the public's interest is renewed and I receive attention, such as requests to speak, sign autographs etc. Competing in the Olympics is not a one-time experience."*

Fellow American Olympian from 1936, **Alice Hodge Arden**, views her Olympic days as exciting and an accomplishment but she too expresses concern about the effect money today has on sport. She says that she would not want to be competing today, and sees the connections she has made both within and outside the sporting world as more important:

*Alice Hodge Arden with her family. Olympic son Russ is behind her (AA)*

> *"Relationships through the years and people I've met have meant more to me than anything. The contacts I have had have been very rewarding. Because my son Russell and I are the only mother and son Olympic relationship (in the US) we get invited everywhere together to different places and I've met all his contemporaries."*

Alice's son, Rusty, went on to achieve great things as a member of the USA Olympic team, and, like Janet Simpson, Rusty competed in Tokyo in 1964.

Some of that Hollywood glitter did rub off on other American competitors. One of the pin-ups of the 1936 games, US fencer **Joanna Harding de Tuscan** had some quite extraordinary experiences afterwards. She turned professional, which she described as 'the greatest favour in the whole world.' She and her husband of the time, Bela de Tuscan, gave a fencing exhibition at the Fox Theatre with Bob Hope which was so successful that they were invited to give shows at all the other Fox Theatres. However, Joanna also experienced the murkier side of show business, when her good looks won her an audition for a leading role in 'Gone With The Wind':

> "My agent Phil Bloom of MCA sent me to have an interview with XX at the Rockefeller Centre in New York. I was ushered past all the people in the waiting room into a very large room. XX greeted me, standing back of his desk. He invited me to come there and sign my contract. When I got to the desk, he unzipped his pants, took out his penis and pointed it at me. I backed away and he followed me. I ran and was trapped in the corner of the room. I stopped and said "Put that thing away. I'm not very big but I am very strong and I will break it in half." He then zipped his pants and took out a large roll of money and offered it to me. I was supposed to sign a contract for the lead (female, of course) in 'Gone with the Wind'. I said I would not sign the contract and he replied that he would keep me locked in the room for three days and that it was sound proof. Well, I signed the contract and went back to Phil Bloom and told him what had happened. His response was that I had to leave the country immediately or I would be sued."

It is worth noting that a couple of the other women included in this book hinted at similar experiences during their sporting careers, but were unwilling to supply details. Joanna and Bela fled the country and performed at the London Palladium. They had a sabre fencing act at a time when women did not fence with sabres.

*"The sabre is much more sensational, all cutting and swinging movements, unlike the close movements of the foil which are not very visible. We were in England for one year. I had shows all over the world, the last in the South Pacific in 1944-45."*

Always ahead of their time, Joanna and Bela invented an electronic method of recording 'hits' in fencing, and Joanna remains an important figure in the development of women's fencing. She still lives in Los Angeles.

*Joanna Harding de Tuscan with her daughter Candice (JH)*

# EN GARDE!

*Joanna de Tuscan advertising Camels cigarettes for Reynolds Tobacco Company 1937 (MF)*

Fellow American, **Gertrude Wilhelmsen Stelling**, says that her life did not change in any way as a result of being Olympian, though she was treated like 'royalty' when she first returned from Berlin in 1936. Gertie maintained her interest in sports, playing basketball, softball and golf to a high standard.

Gertie was one of the very few women to have been married when she competed in Berlin, and the importance of her husband's support throughout her life shines through in her letters.

*"In golf I have made five hole-in-ones in regulation play. One day in a seniors golf tournament in Palm Springs I had five gold medals around my neck and my wonderful husband had happy tears in his eyes and so did I."*

*Portrait of Gertrude Wilhelmsen Stelling for her 85th birthday (GW)*

For the German women who took part in the 1936 Olympics, the Games were a passport to glory in their own country. Although inevitably the War changed things for them, **Trudi Baier Mayer, Elfriede Rahn-Kaun** and **Tilly Gröte Fleischer** have all since met up again at events organised by the German Olympic Association. All three felt that their achievements were recognised and honoured by the German people. Elfriede said:

*Elfriede Rahn-Kaun (left) and Tilly Gröte Fleischer (right) with a friend at a reunion dinner (TFG)*

*"When I came home my life changed. I was suddenly famous and very much admired."*

Gymnast Trudi married a silver medal-winning water polo player and worked as a gym instructor. She is bemused by the high-profile achievements of gymnasts today:

*"The development of the Olympic Games has gone to such lengths nowadays, that none of our age can ever imagine having taken part."*

Tilly made a clear decision to give up athletics because she felt that her last throw in Berlin was her best. She had fulfilled her ambition, and had nothing else to achieve in athletics. Like Elfriede, Tilly's javelin throwing made her famous throughout Germany. She married a dentist and still lives in the Black Forest. The 1936 Olympic champion and world record holder in the discus, Gisela Mauermayer, was a very great and dear friend:

> *"Gisela died in 1996 and was a magnificent human being, honest, fair minded and unique. We must all certainly pass on and Gisela went ahead of me. Everything is as it should be - for sixty years we had a wonderful time in sport and in our personal relationship. My husband died in 1970. Now I live in a beautiful house, and live with my daughter, also called Gisela, who is now sixty one years of age. I have two grandchildren and two great grand children. We are a very happy family. I will soon be eighty eight so I have had a long life!"*

*Dorothy Tyler Odam (SD, AT)*

Whilst Tilly, Elfriede and Trudi were much feted in Germany, the situation in Great Britain was completely different, as **Dorothy Tyler Odam** remembers:

*"When I came back from the Olympics in 1936, no one was interested. A few neighbours asked me how I got on. It didn't mean very much even to me. I was used to winning so I probably was a bit disappointed that I only got silver and I didn't get gold. I didn't realise then how much it would mean in the future not to have won gold. In 1939 I broke the world record in the middle of a school field. Even then I only got two lines in the Stop Press. I think there would have been more about it if I had been a man. Women weren't given much press coverage."*

Dorothy was active during the War, and afterwards took up athletics training again - with further success at the 1948 Olympics in London, though at first it seemed she would be unlikely to make the team:

> *"I had been in the War in the WAAF and I'd come out and started training and had a baby - and I wasn't even on the 'possibles' list. I wasn't getting the (food) parcels, although I was getting extra rations after I won the Championship. My husband used to go and get them - they'd give him more than me because he was a man! I felt it was such a great achievement to come from nothing and then break the Olympic record and jump higher than I'd ever jumped before. As in 1936, I jumped the same height as the winner."*

But once again, Dorothy took silver. High jump rules had changed and the irony was that the new rule added for the 1948 Olympics took into account the number of failures an athlete had in the event of a tied final height. This change in regulations would have ensured gold for Dorothy in 1936. In 1948, the new rule deprived her of that elusive Olympic first place, but she could have won under the old system! Dorothy's amazing athletics career did not end there and she competed in two more Olympics - Helsinki in 1952 and Melbourne in 1956. She even changed her style of jumping from the traditional scissors to the Babe Didrickson style Western Roll:

*"By 1956, I think people thought I was getting too old. A lot of people said 'It's time you gave it up.' My reply was 'While I can travel the world jumping over a high jump bar I shall go on jumping over a high jump bar.' If I'd been earning money it would have been very different. They would have been saying 'You go on while you can still get it.' It would have been a job rather than a career."*

*Dorothy performing Western Roll (DT)*

Dorothy was the first woman to qualify in Great Britain as a jumps coach, and coached several athletes to international honours. She gave much of her life to athletics and it is an extraordinary omission that her work for British athletics has never been recognised by the British Honours System.

Dorothy has recently learned to swim, having been told that it was bad for her high jumping when she was younger, and she plays a lot of golf with a best handicap of ten. With her exceptional athletic ability and dedication, what does she think about sports today?

*"I don't know if I would want to be competing today. All my Olympics career I made friends and we were happy. I was never at loggerheads with my team mates who were competing in the same event."*

Although Dorothy might not want to compete now, it is highly unlikely that today she would remain so overlooked. With her level of commitment and outstanding ability in her sport, Dorothy would undoubtedly have a higher profile as a competitor in modern athletics.

*Audrey Court Brown and her brother Godfrey (AC)*

Dorothy was not the only 1936 athletics team member to continue giving as much as she could to her sport. **Audrey Court Brown** captained the British Women's Team for the European Championships in Vienna in 1938:

*"It was again a rather unhappy political situation and we went with the promise of diplomatic protection if necessary. The political atmosphere in Berlin was nothing like as bad as that in Vienna in 1938 (it was the year Austria allowed herself to be taken over by the Germans and by September they were dearly regretting this). We were in the city when traffic was changed from left to right and when the German Government was making not-so-secret preparations for war and Chamberlain was plucking his nettles! It was an intense relief to know that we had diplomatic protection as we were a small and vulnerable group of women, asked by the Foreign Office to compete as arranged.*

*Immediately after the Championships I took up an appointment at Rowntrees in York, as a Personnel Officer. I kept up with athletics on a less serious scale and also helped some girls who were interested in training. The outbreak of war and marriage in 1940 ended all this. I did nothing in athletics until Dorothy Nelson-Neal dragged me back to serve on the Committee of the Midland Counties Women's AAA for some time and I was President one year."*

The two British gymnasts, **Edna Gross Earl** and **Brenda Halligan Crowe** led quite different lives after their Berlin experience. Edna went as an International Judge to the Helsinki Olympics and coached the British team for the 1956 Olympics in Melbourne. She also taught dancing. Her husband, Leonard was as enthusiastic about gymnastics as Edna, and he was secretary of the Amateur Gymnastics Association (Southern Counties). Edna became ill during 1998 and died on September 18th 1999. Her niece, Mary Evans said:

*"Edna and Leonard never had a family - gymnastics really was their lives and it was more prestigious then than it is now. So few people ever went to the Olympics and I think, for my Aunt, it was incredibly special."*

An article published about Edna in a magazine elicited a response from an ex-pupil, Maureen Whitaker:

> *"Back in the 1940s I actually attended the dancing school Edna ran in Chingford. Her enthusiasm really was an inspiration. It meant so much to me to remember this wonderful lady who gave me such a love of dancing."*

Edna seems to have left quite a mark on those with whom she came into contact and Maureen Whitaker's words are a fine tribute to Edna's life work.

*Brenda Halligan Crowe, summer 1999 (BH)*

Brenda Halligan Crowe has devoted much of her life to her large family. She has continued to be physically active, and when we went to meet her, we mistook her for her daughter, because she looks in such great shape! Although she did not remain in gymnastics as long as Edna did, it would seem that Brenda is one of the few sportswomen of her generation who would not mind competing today:

*"I have a big family with grandchildren and great grandchildren. Although I sometimes feel tired, I really enjoy my garden and walking my dog. The build up to my time at the Olympics was fantastic - I'll never forget it. My worry these days is all the money involved in sport. It's not the same - but the gymnastics these days is absolutely wonderful, and I'd have quite liked to have had a go!"*

In Greece, **Domnitsa Cavanidou Lanitou's** life was hugely affected by the war. She became a nurse in a military hospital, and, during the Occupation, says that her only thought was of survival. She married and had a child and, after the war, began to train again. She was the only Greek woman to compete in the London Olympic Games of 1948. Her experience led to her being elected to the Committee of the Greek Federation for Women's Sports, of which she became President. She headed womens teams that went abroad, and was also a sports journalist:

> *"Unfortunately, I lost my husband too early, twenty seven years ago, and I live alone, having the company of my younger sister, also a widow, and of course my son and his family. I have two grandchildren whom I adore, a boy of thirteen and a girl of six, whom I believe will follow my steps! The press and media generally are still interested in my athletic life of the past, and very*

*often I am asked to give lectures or interviews on television. The Greek state and the Cyprus state have both honoured me as the first (Greek) woman athlete in the Olympics. I have now more than fifty awards, seventeen cups, plaques, diplomas, and prizes of different sorts awarded to me over the last twenty years!"*

*Domintsa Cavanidou Lanitou being presented to the Greek Association of Sports Journalists by the President of the Greek Olympic Association in 1996 (DC)*

Like Domnitsa, **Evelyn Whillier de Lacy** from Australia was planning to enter the 1940 Olympics, but the war thwarted her ambition. Evelyn had a lot of success at the British Empire Games of 1938, winning gold in the 110 yards freestyle, silver in the freestyle relay, and bronze in the medley relay. She cites these as her greatest swimming achievements. Evelyn had three children and her two daughters competed for Australian swimming titles. Evelyn taught swimming for forty six years and still swims, saying that she will continue until called by 'the fellow upstairs'. Evelyn shares the older women's worries about the Olympic movement of today, and looking back says:

*"That time in Berlin was an amazing experience for an eighteen year old from a country area. We were a very naive group of girls coming from so far away from Europe, but we were treated well and learned a lot about life. My life changed after my Olympic experience. I went away mentally a child and came back mentally a woman. I am disappointed with the Olympic Games these days.*

*It's become a corporate affair, it's too expensive for ordinary Australians. I'll be very happy to see the end of it, as I believe the Olympic movement will collapse within itself."*

## Renewing Old Links

High jumper **Doris Carter** also learned a lot about life during her trip with the other three Australian women members of the Olympic team. She remembered getting on 'famously' as a foursome, but they went their separate ways after the Games. In her last letter to us, Doris said that she sincerely hoped "Sydney's games are a great success." Doris lived for the last twelve years in a cottage in a retirement village on the outskirts of Melbourne. After receiving a letter from Evelyn, we sent Doris her address and it was Doris who in turn put us in touch with Pat Down Norton, the 'baby' of the team. We corresponded fairly regularly with Doris but became concerned when we did not receive a reply to a couple of letters. Her nieces, Christine Duggan and Jan Carter, phoned to tell us that Doris had died on July 28th 1999. Doris was the only one of the thirty two Olympic women we contacted never to have married, but she

*Doris Carter leading Melbourne's Anzac Day Parade in 1996 (DC)*

had clearly been very close to her nieces. Christine and Jan went on to tell us many things that their modest aunt had never mentioned to us.

During the 1930s, Doris played hockey for Australia and was the General Manager of the Australian Women's Team at the Melbourne Olympics of 1956. A Wing Officer and Director of the Women's RAAF, she was the first woman to fly in both the Canberra Bomber and the Vampire Jet, and was also the first woman on an Australian war ship. Her proudest moment was in 1996 when she co-led the Melbourne Anzac Day parade. She also held the Order of the British Empire. It was another sad day when we realised that we would not receive any more of Doris' wonderful, vibrant letters, nor get the chance to meet her as we had hoped.

*Fernanda Dobile Bullano (FB)*

Italian sprinter **Fernanda Dobile Bullano** lives alone and is a widow. She says that the memories of her sporting period make her feel 'melancholic'. She regards this time in her life as difficult after the pleasure and responsibility of competing for 'my country, my society, my family and myself'. Fernanda, like many of the women, has a strong sense of family and her duty to society. In 1935, she was affected personally by politics when she had to donate all her athletics medals to the Italian government who were raising revenue to subsidise the war in Abyssinia (Ethiopia). One of the medals had been given to her personally by Mussolini - who then wanted it back! She expresses a lot of sadness about their loss:

> *"My sports club made us give our medals for our country. I have the receipts from the Banque d'Italia dated 27/12/35."*

Fernanda continued to be involved in athletics and became an athletics official until retiring in 1968. Most of the women in this book are now widows. Like Fernanda, **Jeanette Morven Campbell** has lost her husband and speaks of

*Jeanette Morven Campbell at her gransons wedding 1997, Roberto is on the right (JC)*

how hard life is now her long standing partner is no longer with her. Roberto had been a fellow swimmer and became a member of the IOC before his death in 1999. He and Jeanette were successful all over South America during the late 1930s. They had four children, one of whom, Susana Norma, was also an Olympic swimmer in 1964 at the Tokyo Olympics. Jeanette spent many years supporting the efforts to rid Argentina of polio - efforts that have finally paid off. She now lives in an apartment overlooking the Belgrano Athletic Club, and an indoor swimming pool was opened with her name on it. In a letter in 1999, she spoke of her deep friendship with **Pat Down Norton** from Australia:

> *"I became so friendly with Pat, as you can imagine. I loved her. Not having met her for sixty three years, we still wrote to each other for Christmas."*

Pat meanwhile was busy taking up new challenges in Australia. She became an aircraft pilot for a couple of years, then at the age of fifty nine took up gliding. Speaking of her love of flying and life, she said:

*"I prefer an engine! At sixty nine, went white water rafting, ended up under the boat but survived, and at seventy nine decided to amuse myself by trying to put pen to paper.*

*I have a new computer and it does wondrous things, but I'm wanting to throw the damn thing out of the window! Now at eighty... have become schizophrenic... think I'm thirty and the mirror tells me I'm every bit of eighty!"*

Pat and Jeanette had lost touch when we first contacted them. One morning, two letters arrived for us in the same post, one

*Pat Down Norton standing in front of the Olympic Autograph board at Olympic Headquarters in Sydney (PD)*

from Pat and one from Jeanette - somehow, they both thought the other had died. We were delighted to refute the notion and to put them back in contact with each other.

The thirty two women in this book describe much of their Olympic experience with one voice - they say that the Olympics broadened their lives and all felt pride and deep emotion as representatives of their countries. After the Games many devoted their themselves to their families and sacrificed further sporting and professional ambitions. They tell us that life was like that in those days. They cannot imagine having the celebrity status that modern Olympians enjoy and many say that they would not want it. Today, they contend with losing life-long partners and the inescapable process of ageing, as we all must do eventually. But what makes these women outstanding is that, against the odds, they went to the Olympic Games. Their spirits and ideals brought them together to strive to do the very best they could - but in friendship with each other.

We hope that like Pat and Jeanette, many of them will be able to renew their unique Olympic friendships this Millennium, at the dawning of the next century of women in the Olympic Games.

# Postscript

It was Christmas 1997 when our phone rang.

*"Hello, I'm Violet Simpson. I got a letter from you for Violet Webb
and had to think for a moment who it was!"*

She laughed. We were thrilled when Vi told us that she still had all her medals and kit from her athletics days in the thirties. We could hardly wait for Christmas to be over so that we could make the journey to her house to meet her. We were not to be disappointed. Vi had taken the trouble to lay out all her memorabilia on a grand piano, including her much loved British running vest, and she entertained us with her stories of the early days of women's athletics and 'those awful hurdles'.

As we left her house, Vi said that the one person she had longed to meet was Britain's 1992 Olympic gold medalist in the 400 metres hurdles, Sally Gunnell. By one of those extraordinary twists of fate, we knew that Sally's Fit Stop Gym was opening the following week, and we were able to arrange a meeting. In fact, Sally was so interested that she asked Vi to open the gym alongside her. It was an occasion to which Vi, looking considerably younger than her eighty three years, rose with the style of a very Great Lady. As Vi's minders for the day, we basked in the reflected glory as Vi enthralled people with her photographs, medals and memories.

We stayed in touch with Vi over the next year, and she encouraged us with a will in our attempts to get TV companies interested in telling the tale of these formidable women. She even called it our 'Olympic effort'! It took a year for us eventually to find a company willing to film Great Britain's oldest women Olympians - but it was too late for our dear Vi. Shortly before the camera crew took to the road, our worst fear came true, and Vi died on May 27th 1999.

We have been blessed to have been in contact with so many wonderful women Olympians throughout the world who seem to share something beyond their sport - a real love and zest for life. Vi had gallons of that love and life, and so it is to Violet Simpson-Webb that we particularly dedicate this book, with grateful thanks for having known you.

Violet

# APPENDIX

Listed are all the women featured in this book, their country of origin, date of birth (and, in some cases, death) and Olympic events. Married names are given before their names as single women.

## ARGENTINA

**Jeanette Morven Campbell** born 8th March 1916, San Jean de Lous, France. 100 metres Freestyle silver medalist, 1936 Berlin Olympics

## AUSTRALIA

**Edith Frances Payne Robinson** born 26th September 1906, Sydney. 100 Metres and 800 Metres, 1928 Amsterdam Olympics

**Doris Carter** born 5th January 1912, Melbourne, died 28th July 1999. High Jump 1936 Berlin Olympics

**Philomena (Bonnie) Alecia Johnston Mealing** born 18th May 1913. Silver medal 100 Metres Backstroke Los Angeles 1932, set two World Records. Also competed in Amsterdam 1928 Olympics

**Evelyn Whillier de Lacy** born 21st November 1917, Maylands, Perth. Freestyle swimmer, 1936 Berlin Olympics

**Pat Down Norton** born 20th March 1919, Sydney. 100 Metres Backstroke, 1936 Berlin Olympics

## CANADA

**Eva Spinks Dawes** born 27th March 1912, Toronto. Bronze medal in High Jump 1932 Los Angeles Olympics

## GERMANY

**Leni Thymm Junker** born 8th December 1905, Wilhelmshaven, died 9th February 1997. 100 Metres and 4x100 metres Relay, Bronze Medal Relay, 1928 Amsterdam Olympics

**Elfriede Rahn-Kaun** born 5th October 1914, Kiel. Bronze Medal in High Jump, 1936 Berlin Olympics

**Tilly Gröte Fleischer** born 2nd October 1911, Frankfurt, Gold Medal 1936 Berlin Olympics and Bronze Medal, 1932 Los Angeles Olympics, Javelin

**Trudi Baier Meyer** born 13th July 1914, Hanover, Gold medal, 1936 Berlin Olympics, Gymnastics Team event

# GREAT BRITAIN

**Violet Simpson Webb** born 3rd February 1915, Willesden, London, died May 27th 1999. 80 metres hurdles finalist, bronze 4x100 relay 1932 Los Angeles Olympics, 80 metres hurdles semi-finalist 1936 Berlin Olympics

**Dorothy Tyler Odam** born 14th March 1920, Clapham, London. High Jump, Silver medals in 1936 Berlin and 1948 London Olympics. Also competed in Helsinki 1952 and 1956 Melbourne Olympics

**Joyce Badcock Cooper** born 18th April 1909, Ceylon. Bronze 100 metres freestyle, bronze 100 metres backstroke, silver 4x100 metres relay 1928 Amsterdam Olympics. Bronze 4 by 100 relay, finalist 100 metres backstroke and 400 freestyle 1932 Los Angeles Olympics

**Sarah (Cissie) Hunt Stewart** born 19th July 1911, Dundee, Scotland. 400 metres freestyle swimmer finalist, 4th, and silver medal 4x100 relay 1928 Amsterdam Olympics.

**Jean Burnett McDowell** born 22nd September 1908, Edinburgh, Scotland. 100 metres freestyle finalist 1928 Amsterdam Olympics *

**Edna Gross Earl** born 12th December 1910 died September 18th 1999 Gymnast 1936 Berlin Olympics

**Brenda Halligan Crowe** born 31st July 1913, Wood Green, London. Gymnast 1936 Berlin Olympics

**Audrey Court Brown** born 24th May 1913, Bengal, India. 100 metres, silver 4x100 metres relay 1936 Berlin Olympics

# GREECE

**Domintsa Cavanidou Lanitis** born 7th January 1916. 80 metres hurdles, 1936 Berlin Olympics and 1948 London Olympics

# HOLLAND

**Wilhelmina Kuyper Duchateau** 9th November 1904 - 28th April 1999. 800 metres, 1928 Amsterdam Olympics, family member, Bill van Dijk, recalled her memories and stories

**Marie Smit Vierdag** born 22nd September 1905. 400 metres freestyle swimmer and 4x100 metres relay 1924 Paris Olympics, 1928 Amsterdam Olympics and 1932 Los Angeles Olympics. Silver medal 1932 4x100 relay

*\* Sadly we have just heard that Jean died on 1st February 2000*

## ITALY

**Matilde Moraschi** born 11th April 1910, Milan. 100 metres, 1928 Amsterdam Olympics

**Vittorina Vivenza Devoti** born 6th June 1912, Villalba. Discus 1928 Amsterdam Olympics

**Fernanda Bullano Dolite** born 26th September 1914, Turin. 100 metres and relay 1936 Berlin Olympics

## SWEDEN

**Maud Elisabeth Nørklit Sundberg** born 22nd December 1911, Stockholm. 100 metres and 4x100 metres relay Amsterdam 1928 Olympics

**Signe Engdahl Johansson** born 27th May 1905. Diver 3 metre spring board 1924 Paris Olympics, 5th

## USA

**Gertrude F. Wilhelmsen Stelling** born 16th January 1913, Puyallup, Washington State. Javelin and Discus 1936 Berlin Olympics

**Alice Jean Hodge Arden** born 23rd July 1914, Philadelphia. High Jump, 1936 Berlin Olympics

**Helen Eileen Carroll Johns** born 25th September 1914, Boston, Massachusetts. Olympic Gold Medalist, Olympic and World record holder in 4x100 Metres Freestyle Swimming Relay 1932 Los Angeles Olympics

**Joanna S. Harding de Tuscan** born 30th April 1908, Detroit. Individual Foil and Captain of USA Fencing team, 1936 Berlin Olympics

**Elizabeth Schwartz Robinson** born 23rd August 1911, Riverdale, Illinois (died May 18th 1999). First woman ever to win a gold medal in the Olympic Games on the track in 100 metres, silver medal in 4x100 metres relay 1928 Amsterdam Olympics. Gold 4x100 metres relay, 1936 Berlin Olympics

**Carol Metten Fletcher** born 22nd November 1907 Denver, Colorado, died 5th April 1998. Diver - Bronze 3 Metre springboard 1924 Paris Olympics

# REFERENCES

## INTRODUCTION

*1*   Wolf Lyberg , 'Fabulous 100 Years of the IOC' (quoting IOC Olympic Review 1912) 1996 p360

## CHAPTER 1 - The Earliest Olympics

### Female Pedestrians

*1*   Peter Lovesey, article 'Women behaving Madly' Inside Track  April 1998. Also see other work by Peter Lovesey

### The Race to Revive the Olympic Games

*1*   Much Wenlock Society Archive, local newspaper

*2*   M.Biddiss, article 'The Sports Lecture:  Stronger, Faster, Higher: The Birth of the Modern Olympics' Sports Historian Vol.50 Spring 1996 p4

*3*   Jennifer Hargreaves, 'Sporting Females'  1994 p45

### Melpomene

*1*   Athanasios Tarasouleas, article 'The Female Spiridon Loues', International Society of Olympic Historians Journal Vol.1 No.3 1993 p11

*2*   Ibid

## CHAPTER 2 - Paris 1900: The First Official Olympic Games for Women

### Croquet

*1*   A.E. Gill, 'Croquet the Complete Guide' 1988 p74

*2*   Maurice Thompson, article 'The Witchery of Archery' p215

### Ballooning

*1*   Mary Henson Leigh, 'The Evolution of Women's Participation in the Summer Olympic Games, 1900-1948', (quoting from 'Chronique du mois' in La Revue Olympique August 1911) 1974 p126-127

### Equestrianism

*1*   Bill Mallon, 'The 1900 Olympic Games - Results for all competitors in all events' 1998

*2*   Louisville Herald, 7th July 1912

## CHAPTER 3 - Preparing for Glory

### Votes and Games For Women

*1*  U. Simri, 'A Historical Analysis of the Role of Women in the Modern Olympic Games' 1977 p5

## CHAPTER 4 - One Step Forward Two Steps Back. 1900-1924

*1*  Mary Henson Leigh, 'The Evolution of Women's Participation in the Summer Olympic Games, 1900-1948' (quoting 'Memoires Olympiques, Lausanne Bureau de Pedagogie Sportive 1931') 1974 p126

### Archery

*1*  E.G.Heath, 'A History of Target Archery' 1973 p76

*2*  1845 Rules of Archery

*3*  E.G.Heath, 'A History of Target Archery' p131

*4*  Ibid p103

### Swimming

*1*  Ian Keil and Don Wix, 'In the Swim: The ASA from 1869-1994' 1996 p40

*2*  Ibid p188

### Gymnastics

*1*  Mary Henson Leigh, 'The Evolution of Women's Participation in the Summer Olympic Games, 1900-1948' p111

*2*  Joyce Godber and Isabel Hutchins, 'A Century of Challenge 1882-1982' 1982 p196

*3*  A. Alexander, 'Drill for The Standards', 1894 p12

*4*  Jim Prestidge, 'The History of British Gymnastics 1888-1988' 1988 p59

### Fencing

*1*  All fencing quotes and references are from Miss Lowther's personal scrap book 1898-1904 in the personal collection of Malcolm Fare

## CHAPTER 5 - The Biggest Hurdle

*1*  Allen Guttman, 'Women's Sports - A History' quoting M. Leigh, 'The Evolution of Women's Participation' 1991 p171

2    R. Gaffner, 'The IOC 100 Years, Women Enter the Stadium' p228

3    F.A.M. Webster, 'Athletics of Today for Women - History, Development and Training' 1930 p101

4    Ibid p102

5    Noel Henry, 'From Sophie to Sonia - a history of women's athletics' 1998 p21

6    Eric L. Cowe, 'Early Women's Athletics: Statistics and History Vol.1' 1999 p118

## CHAPTER 6 - Amsterdam 1928

1    Canadian Olympic Association Handbook of the Olympic Games of 1928 p72

2    Ibid p66

3    Ibid

4    Ibid p67

5    Ibid

6    Ibid p74

7    Ibid p73

8    Ibid p74

9    British Olympic Association Official Report 1928 p147

10   Canadian Olympic Association Handbook of the Olympic Games of 1928 p68

11   British Olympic Association Official Report 1928 p233

12   Ibid p239

13   Ibid p237

14   Fencing Rules 1928, Malcolm Fare

15   Ruud Paauw, article, 'After the Glory' ISOH Journal Vol.2 No.1 Winter 1994

## CHAPTER 7 - Los Angeles 1932

1    Doris H. Pieroth quoting Chicago Tribune, 1st August 1932, 'Their Day in the Sun' 1996 p101

2   Doris H. Pieroth quoting Los Angeles Times, 5th August 1932, 'Their Day in the Sun' p109

3   Stan Greenberg, 'Olympic Facts and Feats' 1996 p32

## CHAPTER 8 - Images of the Berlin Olympics of 1936

1   Karl Lennartz, article 'Hitler's Violation of the Olympic Rules in 1936' ISOH Journal; Vol.2 No.3 Autum 1994, p9. Also see Olympic Apocrypha: The non-snub of 1936, Donald Sayenga (same journal)

2   Tony Bijerk, article 'The Empress of Berlin forgotten, undervalued and still going....but not very strong.' ISOH journal Vol. 5 No.2 Summer 1997 p31

3   Ibid p30

4   Ibid

5   Transcript of Lowell Thomas' Broadcast 24th July 1936, Alice Hodge Arden's private collection

6   For more about Olympic Oaks see 'The 1936 Olympic Oaks: Where Are They Now?' by James Ross Constadt

## CHAPTER 9

1   'The Olympic Review' No.XXVI -15th June/July 1997 p29

2   Joanna Davenport article 'Monique Berliox - Her Association With Three IOC Presidents'. ISOH Journal 'Citius, Altius, Fortius' Autumn 1996 p12

3   Private letter to authors, Daniels and Tedder, 2nd February 1999

4   Fax to Stephanie Daniels from Anita DeFrantz, 31st January 1997

# BIBLIOGRAPHY

Without the work of the following writers this would have been impossible:

**Ian Buchanan**, 'British Olympians: A Hundred Years of Gold Medalists'
*(Guiness Publishing, Enfield 1991)*
**Arthur Lillie**, 'Croquet Up To Date' *(Longman's Green and Co., London 1900)*
**D.M.C. Prichard**, 'The History of Croquet' *(Cassell Ltd., London 1981)*
**A.E. Gill**, 'Croquet, The Complete Guide' *(Heinemann Kingswood, London 1988)*
**Jim Prestidge**, 'The History of British Gymnastics 1888-1988'
*(The British Amateur Gymnastic Association 1988)*
**E.G. Heath**, 'A History of Target Archery' *(David and Charles Ltd, Newton Abbot, Devon 1973)*
**Peter Lovesey**, 'The Official Centenery of the AAA' *(Guiness Superlatives, London 1979)*
**Edwin J. Kirschener**, 'Aerospace Balloons' *(Aero Publishers, Inc. USA 1985)*
**Alex Hay**, 'The Handbook of Golf' *(Pelham Books, London 1984)*
**Ann Holland**, 'Stride by Stride, The Illustrated Story of Horseracing'
*(Macdonald Queen Anne Press, GB 1989)*
**Jeffrey Pearson**, 'Lottie Dod, Champion of Champions' *(Countrywise Ltd. 1988)*
**John Fabb**, 'Flying and Ballooning from Old Photographs' *(B.T. Batsford Ltd. 1980)*
**Malcolm Crane**, 'The Story of Ladies Golf' *(Stanley Paul and Co., London 1991)*
**Jonathan Rice**, 'Start of Play' *(Prion Books, London 1998)*
**Dr Rudolph Brasch**, 'How Did Sports Begin?' *(Tynron Press, Scotland 1990)*
**Stan Cohen**, 'The Games of 36' *(Pictorial Histories, Missoula, Montana 1996)*
**F.A.M. Webster**, 'Athletics of Today For Women' *(Frederick Warne and Co. 1930)*
**Sophie Eliott-Lynn**, 'Athletics For Women and Girls' *(Frederick Warne and Co. 1930)*
**Peter Pozzoli**, 'British Women's Athletics, Part 2 International 1921-1964'
*(Arena Publication 1965)*
**Jennifer Hargreaves**, 'Sporting Females' *(Routledge 1994)*
**Joyce Godber and Isabel Hutchins**, 'A Century of Challenge 1882-1982'
*(Bedford High School 1982)*
**Uriel Simri**, 'A Historical Analysis of the Role of Women in the Modern Olympics' *(Netanya 1977)*
**Ian Keil and Don Wix**, 'In the Swim' *(Swimming times Ltd. 1996)*
**Eric L. Cowe**, 'International Women's Athletics 1890-1940' *(Cowe 1985)*
**Eric L. Cowe**, 'Early Women's Athletics: Statistics and History' *(Cowe 1999)*
**Noel Henry**, 'From Sophie to Sonia: A History of Women's Athletics' *(Noel Henry 1998)*
**Doris H. Pieroth**, 'Their Day in the Sun' *(University of Washington Press 1996)*
**Stan Greenberg**, 'Olympic Facts and Feats' *(Guiness 1996)*
**Bill Mallon**, 'The 1900 Olympic Games: Results for all competitors in all events, with
commentary' *(McFarland and Company Inc. 1998)*
**British Olympic Association Reports 1928, 32 and 36**
**Canadian Olympic Association Report 1928**
**USA Olympic Association Reports 1928, 32 and 36**
**IOC Museum Library and Archives**
**Associated Newspaper Libraries**

Unpublished Theses

**Mary Hanson Leigh**, 'The Evolution of Women's Participation in the Summer Olympic Games
1900-1948' *(Ohio State University 1974)*
**Greg Moon**, 'A New Dawn Rising. An Empirical and Social Study Concerning the Emergence and
Development of English Women's Athletics Until 1980' *(Roehampton Institute London 1997)*

# INDEX

49453

INDEX